UP
RISING

"Kris Vallotton fearlessly addresses the plight of the fatherless through a hope-filled lens of generational reconciliation. This book will leave you equipped and empowered to pursue the Malachi Mandate and join the fight that will impact the here and now while also creating a long-lasting legacy of families with Christ at the center."

Dante Bowe, worship leader and songwriter;
Grammy nominee and Dove Award winner

"As someone who is raising four boys, the call to equip the next generation to walk in godly masculinity is close to my heart. Kris challenges what culture has told us is normal and calls us back to God's design for the family. His message is timely and significant!"

Havilah Cunnington, founder, Truth to Table

"This might be the most important book of the decade. Our true Father is yearning to heal fatherlessness in our world. Let's agree with His plan!"

John Eldredge, bestselling author, *Wild at Heart*

"*Uprising* captures Kris Vallotton's passion for reconciling the generations by connecting fathers to their families at a time when every force of evil is focused on dividing and conquering. With very practical strategies and examples, *Uprising* provides a roadmap where all trails lead home and dads fulfill their God-given purpose."

Jentezen Franklin, senior pastor, Free Chapel;
New York Times bestselling author

"Kris Vallotton calls out fatherlessness as the scourge of our time in this excellent book. He doesn't just identify the problem—he gives real solutions. When I was a police officer in Los Angeles, I saw firsthand the devastation of an entire culture when fathers abandon their role of raising their children. I couldn't agree more with Kris as he calls men back to our mandate of raising the next generation to love and obey God."

Ken Harrison, chairman, Promise Keepers

"The profound message contained in this book has been forming in the heart of my friend the author for many years. I have watched the process with amazement and excitement, knowing it would find its way into print. And while everything Kris has written to date has had a powerful impact on how we think and live, *Uprising* may, in fact, shape us and our nation as much as all the others combined. I hope it does, as it is that important. I don't remember being as excited for the release of another author's book as I am for this one.

"Our world is crying out for answers, all while falling for lies and delusions that bring destruction in the process. Culturally we lack the biblical moorings that anchor a nation in truth. *Uprising* brings us back to our foundations, as it contains the blueprint of heaven for bringing healing to families and, ultimately, the nations of the world. But it starts with the restoration of the individual. And while Kris addresses men and fathers throughout, his message equally benefits women. I pray that this book will circle the world and become the book that politicians, professors, CEOs, religious leaders and leaders in the fields of science and medicine turn to in difficult times. If this book becomes the lens through which people interpret cultural challenges, we will have answers that generate healing, positively affecting multiple generations. Read this book. Prayerfully read this book. And let's see what might happen in our lifetime."

Bill Johnson, Bethel Church, Redding, California;
author, *Open Heavens* and *Born for Significance*

"I have had the honor of knowing the Vallotton family for years. Today, more than ever, we need sons, husbands and fathers who will show Jesus to the world by loving their families. It has been a true privilege to watch Kris serve, lead and love God's family so beautifully."

Michael Koulianos, pastor, Jesus Image

"*Uprising* is not just another book but a message that cuts to the heart and calls us to action. With clarity and conviction, Kris reveals the heart of God for this hour while prophetically and practically inviting us to be a part of His purpose. It is time for fathers to rise up with a passion for sons and daughters. This book will awaken you to God's plan for His children."

Banning Liebscher, founder and pastor, Jesus Culture

"Men of this generation desperately need a wake-up call. In *Uprising*, Kris Vallotton issues the call with compassion and conviction. Alongside his own story, Vallotton shares his heart for this 'fatherless generation' with the courage and commitment of Nehemiah. Readers will receive an education in the current social landscape and practical, biblical principles for joining the uprising God invites us into as men of faith."

Samuel Rodriguez, lead pastor, New Season Worship; president and CEO, National Hispanic Christian Leadership Conference; author, *Persevere with Power*; executive producer, *Breakthrough* and *Flamin' Hot* (movies)

"They say a dad is 'the anchor upon which his children stand.' I can find no truer words for my dad than these. He has been the greatest source of strength in my life and the one man I know I can count on regardless of the situation. From anxiety and depression to addiction, divorce and remarriage, my father gave me the courage to stand when all my hope was lost. Growing up, I assumed every boy had a father like mine who modeled manhood daily. Sadly, this could not be further from the truth. It is my prayer that through this book, my dad's words will impart the same healing and courage into you that have molded the man I am today."

Jason Vallotton, founder, BraveCo; author, *Winning the War Within*

UPRISING

The Epic Battle for the Most
Fatherless Generation in History

KRIS VALLOTTON

Chosen

a division of Baker Publishing Group
Minneapolis, Minnesota

Published by Chosen Books
11400 Hampshire Avenue South
Minneapolis, Minnesota 55438
www.chosenbooks.com

Chosen Books is a division of
Baker Publishing Group, Grand Rapids, Michigan

Printed in the United States of America

Library of Congress Cataloging-in-Publication Data
Names: Vallotton, Kris, author.
Title: Uprising : the epic battle for the most fatherless generation in history / Kris Vallotton.
Description: Minneapolis, Minnesota : Chosen Books, a division of Baker Publishing Group, [2022] | Includes bibliographical references.
Identifiers: LCCN 2022002361 | ISBN 9780800762735 (cloth) | ISBN 9781493439232 (ebook) | ISBN 9780800763077 (trade paper)
Subjects: LCSH: Families—Religious aspects—Christianity. | Fatherhood—Religious aspects—Christianity. | Paternal deprivation—Religious aspects—Christianity. | Absentee fathers. | Fatherless families.
Classification: LCC BV4526.3 .V35 2022 | DDC 248.4—dc23/eng/20220225
LC record available at https://lccn.loc.gov/2022002361

Unless otherwise indicated, Scripture quotations are from the (NASB®) New American Standard Bible®, Copyright © 1960, 1971, 1977, 1995 by The Lockman Foundation. Used by permission. All rights reserved. www.lockman.org

Scripture quotations identified ESV are from The Holy Bible, English Standard Version® (ESV®), copyright © 2001 by Crossway, a publishing ministry of Good News Publishers. Used by permission. All rights reserved. ESV Text Edition: 2016

Scripture quotations identified NIV are from THE HOLY BIBLE, NEW INTERNATIONAL VERSION®, NIV® Copyright © 1973, 1978, 1984, 2011 by Biblica, Inc.® Used by permission. All rights reserved worldwide.

Scripture quotations identified NKJV are from the New King James Version®. Copyright © 1982 by Thomas Nelson. Used by permission. All rights reserved.

Cover design by LOOK Design Studio

Baker Publishing Group publications use paper produced from sustainable forestry practices and post-consumer waste whenever possible.

22 23 24 25 26 27 28   7 6 5 4 3 2 1

I dedicate this book to

My father, Bill Vallotton,
who passed away when I was three years old. I know you are
watching me from heaven. I have carried you in
my heart my whole life.

Art Kipperman,
my first spiritual father, who taught me how to follow Jesus.
I miss you!

Bill Derryberry,
who has discipled me for the last forty years and taught me how to
be a man. I live forever in your debt.

Bill Johnson,
who has inspired and empowered me to change the world!
Thank you for believing in me before I deserved it.

My heavenly Father,
who has loved me and protected me my whole life.
My prayer is that I would be a blessing to You, and that
You would be proud to call me Your son.

The Malachi Mandate

Behold, I will send you Elijah the prophet before the great and awesome day of the LORD comes. And he will turn the hearts of fathers to their children and the hearts of children to their fathers, lest I come and strike the land with a decree of utter destruction.

Malachi 4:5–6 ESV

CONTENTS

INTRODUCTION

In some ways, I have been preparing to write this book for most of my life. My father drowned when I was three years old, and I have spent much of my life longing for him. The truth is, I never really understood what I was longing for until our first child, Jaime, turned four years old. I will never forget that moment. I was pushing her down a hill on her tricycle, and we both were laughing wildly. Suddenly, this thought came to my mind: *My daddy was gone by this time in my life. There was no laughter in my life at four years old, only loneliness and confusion.*

Every day since that tricycle ride has been a continued revelation of my life, absent of fatherhood. I am 66 years old at the writing of this book, and I can't remember a day when I didn't miss my dad. Every time I have had a crisis in my life, I have had the thought, *I wish my dad were here. He would know what to do.* My office is filled with mementos of places I've been, books I've written and things I've accomplished. On the entry wall of my office is a picture of my dad. I hung it there strategically so I could remind myself that my father would be proud of me if he could see the man I've become.

We live in the most fatherless generation in the history of the world. For me, this statement isn't just a commentary on society; it's personal . . . painfully personal! Over half of the children in America today are born out of wedlock . . . left alone, with no daddy! Furthermore, there's an entire movement that is trying to "normalize" having two mommies and no daddy, or having two daddies and no mommy. It's hard to stand by in silence when you have lived the deep pain of a dysfunctional family and understand the plight of losing a parent. Yet our society is trying to normalize brokenness that's so deep it defies logical explanation. The hope is that normalizing immoral lifestyles will remove the intense shame of living in sin.

> ## We live in the most fatherless generation in the history of the world.

That's like saying if people would stop shaming you for smoking, then you wouldn't get lung cancer. Society has become convinced that the guilt of immorality is externally generated and will lift when the world around immoral people agrees with their behavior. Yet Jesus said that the Holy Spirit is the one who convicts the world from the inside out. Read it for yourself:

> But I tell you the truth, it is to your advantage that I go away; for if I do not go away, the Helper will not come to you; but if I go, I will send Him to you. And He, when He comes, will convict the world concerning sin and righteousness and judgment.
>
> John 16:7–8

In other words, we can run, but we can't hide.

The Malachi Mandate

In the book of Nehemiah, the walls of Jerusalem had been broken down for 141 years, and the Jews had been unsuccessful in rebuilding the walls for 94 years. But what the Israelites couldn't do in 94 years, Nehemiah did in 52 days!

How did he do it? you ask. That's a great question. First, he surveyed the walls and developed a strategy to rebuild them. But what he did next is stunning. He made the reconstruction of the walls a family affair! He put families to work together on the section of the wall closest to their houses. One day, half of each family worked on the wall near them, while the other half protected their workers with weapons of warfare. The next day the halves would switch, and the family members who had posted guard duty the day before would work on the wall, while those who had worked the day before would protect the family workers.

Like Nehemiah, in this book I will first survey the broken walls of this generation. I will describe the side effects of what has become the new PC (politically correct) culture, along with looking at the resultant deconstruction of the family unit. But the ultimate purpose of this book is to inspire the Malachi Mandate—to build bridges of reconciliation between the generations that will facilitate the restoration of fathers and their families.

> The ultimate purpose of this book is to inspire the Malachi Mandate—to build bridges of reconciliation between the generations that will facilitate the restoration of fathers and their families.

ONE

Where It All Began

LEWISTON IS A TINY TOWN of 900 people nestled in the Trinity Alps of California. A single subdivision is home to about 750 Lewiston residents. This subdivision was built in 1960 to house the laborers who worked on the Lewiston Dam project. A couple of decades later, Lewiston became a breeding ground for drugs and prostitution, drawing many kids and teenagers into its clutches, ultimately stealing their innocence and destroying their purity. Consequently, what looked like a sleepy, peaceful mountain community on the outside was a town steeped in addiction and wallowing in abuse and dysfunction.

The Trinity County Probation Department became so inundated with the impact this community was having on the entire county that its workers decided to become proactive and go after the root system of brokenness. They discovered in their analysis that all the juveniles on probation in Trinity County came from shattered families. Furthermore, a high percentage of the juveniles in Lewiston had violated their probation. Based on these findings, the probation department decided to make a decree that *all the parents* of kids who had violated probation would be required to take a parenting class twice a week for three months, or they would face their children going back to juvenile hall.

17

This is where my story begins. Because I was a volunteer youth pastor for nine years at Mountain Chapel, I came to know Dick, the head of the probation department. I had stepped aside from the youth pastor role for about a year and was waiting for a new assignment from the Lord. Dick called me one winter day during this time, in November 1987, and said, "Kris, I'm requiring the parents of all the juvenile probation violators to take a three-month parenting class. It's twice a week, on Tuesdays and Thursdays. I was hoping you could work with the kids while my team does some parenting classes with their folks. I'll get you access to the old gym in Lewiston; maybe you could do some activities with the kids and then share a positive message with them a couple of times a week. And Kris, I know you're a Christian, but I can't have you banging the kids with the Bible because I'm requiring them to come to your meeting. You know about the separation of church and state stuff, right, buddy?"

"Yeah, Dick . . . well, this could be amazing! Okay, I'll do it," I responded.

Honestly, I had *no idea* what I had just said yes to! That week, I got the keys to the old, dilapidated gym, which hadn't been opened in years. It had no insulation, leaked like a sieve in the rain and had no heat or air conditioning. I unlocked the huge metal double doors and forced them open against their rusty hinges as they groaned in protest. Then I stood in the doorway and tried to absorb the scene in front of me. The place was *filled* with spiderwebs hanging everywhere, like a horror scene in a haunted house movie. The floor was covered in dirt, and garbage was slung all over the place. Bird crap ran down the walls like rain as rats scurried for cover. The stench of rat feces rolled out of the doorway like cigarette smoke.

> Honestly, I had *no idea* what I had just said yes to!

"Yikes!" I said out loud, trying to prepare my family, who were in tow, for the view ahead. Kathy and the kids joined me in the doorway in complete silence. Frankly, I was afraid to ask them what they were thinking . . . or maybe it was just that I could read the sense of utter surprise on their faces. Whatever the case, we all grabbed brooms and went to work. We spent the next couple of weeks cleaning out the gym, making it ready for its maiden voyage.

18

Gym 1.0

Finally, the big day arrived. Kathy baked cookies and brought enough soda for 35 kids (the number we were told to expect). We loaded up our three kids (thirteen, eleven and nine years old) and headed for the gym. The 30-minute ride there was unusually quiet; you could cut the anxiety in the car with a knife. Somehow, in spite of the dark cloud that settled on us, I had a vivid, fictitious story come to my mind on the way there about the value of virginity.

We arrived at the gym, but there was no way to prepare for what we were about to experience. We got there 20 minutes early, yet there were already kids waiting to get in. I wasn't sure what their expectation was for the night or if they even knew who we were, but we were about to find out. I greeted them with a "Yo!" that they ignored completely. I promptly unlocked the gym door, and they rushed in like a bunch of wild animals, pushing and shoving each other to get in first, nearly ripping the doors off their hinges. They passed me as if I were invisible, practically running over my kids and me. "Yikes!" I gasped again.

We had wanted to be there early enough to set up the gym with games and organize the night, but the waiting kids trampled that plan in the first few minutes. I tried desperately to get their attention and give them some brief instructions for the evening, but they just flipped me off and yelled obscenities at my family and me. Kathy ignored their insults, grabbed a volleyball and organized a game on the fly. I followed suit, brought out a basketball (which attracted their attention like moths to a flame) and tried to create some structure.

It was a zoo! A few minutes after our arrival, two teenagers got into a full-on fistfight, surrounded by kids yelling and screaming at them. I shouted at the top of my lungs for them to *STOP!* But it was no use. I was nearly paralyzed with fear. My heart was pounding, sweat poured down my face and my hands shook in terror. But there was no one there to bail us out. We were 30 minutes into the first night, and the kids had literally taken over the building. Somehow, I had to take control and turn this whole thing around before it was too late. I rushed into the fight and managed to get both guys in a headlock and wrestle them to the ground, pinning them to the floor. For the first time, the gym went completely silent.

"Listen to me," I said, struggling to hold both guys on the ground. "This stops *now*, or you can take your skinny little butts home and fight in your driveway. This is my gym, and if you want it open, then we play by my rules—or I lock the freakin' place up and never come back. *Is that clear?*"

There was no reply, but the silence was encouraging. I let the two tough guys go. They both jumped to their feet, staring at each other right in the eyes, as if to taunt one another. I got between them and shouted, "*Knock it off or get out of my gym NOW!*" A few seconds later, they were back in the basketball game. (But I would break up five more fights before the night was over.)

Finally, it was "halftime," and we gathered up the balls and demanded that everyone sit on the benches assembled against one wall of the gym. We bribed the kids with cookies and drinks. They shouted obscenities at us in return and screamed, "*How long is this going to take? Hey, man, what's going on? . . . Let's play ball . . . what the %@$&*!*"

By some near miracle, we managed to get the 37 kids who had shown up seated. I immediately started telling the fictitious story the Lord had given me on the way to the gym about a teenager who worked for a ring for "the woman of his dreams."[1] For the first five minutes, the kids cussed, sneered and harassed me while I struggled to recount the story. But then suddenly, something happened. Somehow they got into the story, and the place became completely silent.

I continued with the story about how this guy worked all through high school, six days a week, for three years to buy this ring for "the woman of his dreams." I wove the ring story around the young man who worked and fought for the ring, even taking it with him to the Vietnam War, in which he was nearly killed trying to retrieve it from the battlefield. The 20-minute story climaxed with the guy finally marrying "the woman of his dreams" and presenting her with the ring on their honeymoon night.

The next morning, however, this newlywed wife lost the ring by carelessly wearing it in the ocean where they went swimming. The young wife couldn't understand her new husband's complete brokenness over the loss. She had come from a rich family, and she thought the value of the ring was in the gold and the diamonds. What she didn't understand was that the true value of the ring was in the blood, sweat and tears it had taken her new husband to get the ring from the battlefield all the way to the honeymoon suite, so that on the night he first lay with his lover he had something valuable to give her. Because anyone can give away something expensive, but only those who understand sacrifice can give away something truly valuable.

Here comes the punch line I delivered to that gym full of tough teens: "The ring is your virginity, and the reason you have a sex drive years before God wants you to have sex inside marriage is because the value of your virginity is in the battle it takes to get your virginity from the battlefield all the way to the honeymoon suite."

At that point, every kid in the gym was hanging his or her head, and their tears fell to the gym floor like rain. A few seconds passed before, finally, the toughest kid in the gym (the instigator of most of the fights that night) broke the silence. He said in a sad voice, "No one ever %#$*&@ told me about this!"

A sixteen-year-old girl who had been behaving seductively all night shouted, "Me neither!"

> **Anyone can give away something expensive, but only those who understand sacrifice can give away something truly valuable.**

The other kids just moaned in agreement as we all sat there in silence. I didn't know how to close the message since I had been forbidden to give an "altar call."

The kids got up from the benches and started playing again, and although they still cussed, yelled and even fought the rest of the night, there was a noticeable crack in their armor. I can't really describe it, but I could feel it in the air. I knew that God had given us these kids, and I was convinced that, in time, we were going to make a huge impact on them.

When the night was finally over, I locked the gym doors over the protests of the kids, and we began our journey home. Our car was buzzing with conversation as everyone told "war stories" of our first night from hell (or a tough night from heaven). The jury was out!

When Thursday rolled around, fear gripped my soul as I envisioned another out-of-control night with our gang of juvenile delinquents. I wondered how we were going to endure three months of sheer trauma, yet I was determined to keep my word to Dick. We arrived at the gym and found the same familiar scene as the first time—except that there were twice as many kids waiting to get in the doors. I reassured myself that we knew what to expect and that we mustn't let the kids take control of the night. I told my family that we needed to be much firmer, but still be loving and compassionate.

As soon as we turned the lights on, the place went ballistic with energy . . . kids shouting, running around chasing each other, the overall feeling of chaos back in full force. We somehow managed to organize a full-court game of basketball (more like jungle ball), with about twenty people on the court at any given time, and a volleyball game with the same sort of overcrowded scenario. The arguing and fighting continued as we worked to build a connection with the kids. I picked out the five oldest, toughest kids in the building and determined to build trust with them. There was no way to develop a quick connection with that many broken and unruly kids, but all the kids respected (mostly feared) these five older kids.

The group grew larger every week, and several older, gangster-looking twentysomethings joined us. The rough-and-tumble dynamic continued, and my concern and fear escalated as I began to see drug deals going down in the gym and guys carrying weapons. At last, our three-month commitment was over. But personally, I was just beginning to bond with the kids. Furthermore, there were at least a hundred kids a night coming to the gym. I reasoned, *Without the probation department's oversight, my 30-minute inspirational talks could include Jesus messages and altar calls.* I talked to Dick and asked him if I could continue meeting with the kids at the gym on my own. He was excited about me continuing, as long as I took full responsibility for the gatherings.

The next week, I invited my five older tough kids to a meeting and pitched them an idea. (I asked these guys to meet with me because all the other kids respected them.) I told them I would continue to open the gym twice a week, providing that they policed the nights. I said, "You guys have to keep the drugs and weapons out of the gym, and you must break up all the fights. If there's one more drug deal in or around the gym, or if anyone brings another weapon into the gym, I am done *forever*! You understand this?"

"Yeah, dude . . . we get it." They shrugged and began to walk away.

"Yo, guys, do we have a deal or not?" I pressed. "I want your word . . . you have mine."

They looked at each other and nodded yes.

"Is that a *YES*? I want you to give me your word," I insisted.

"Yeah, dude, we're in," they said with sarcastic smirks on their faces. (I honestly don't think these kids had ever been trusted before, so they weren't quite sure how to respond.)

When we are leading people (especially broken people), it's important that we set well-articulated boundaries with them and clearly communicate the ramifications of violating those expectations. In this case, the risk of having kids with guns, knives and drugs in the gym, with no security or police protection present, was incredibly dangerous. We had to find a solution that really worked, and I knew how much these guys were loving the gatherings at the gym, so I was pretty confident they would do anything to keep it open.

Gym 2.0

My hunch turned out to be right. The next Tuesday, we opened the gym, and I gathered everyone around me as the five tough kids I had met with shouted for everyone to "*Shut the %@$&* up!*" It wasn't quite the opening I had in mind, but I have to say, it was effective. I shared the new deal with everyone and made it clear that they *must* police the gym themselves or I was *gone forever*!

Everything changed that day, although it took about a year to completely eradicate the attempts to bring in drugs and weapons. When new people came into the building and tried to do a drug deal with our kids, the tough guys would gather around them and usher them out of the gym. The kids created a place off the premises to hide their drugs and weapons, so they could ditch them there, come in and play ball.

At halftime, the kids could grab some snacks, sit on the benches and listen to me teach, or they could go outside for 30 minutes, until I was done. Snacks were included either way. At first, about 70 percent of them went outside with the "cool kids" and listened at the open windows (actually, the air vents). But the first snow drove them all inside, and from then on, even the cool kids stayed in the gym year-round. They grew to like my teaching (even though they tried not to show it). I was teaching them practical life skills, along with the Gospel. Little by little, we were becoming one big (slightly dysfunctional) family.

> They grew to like my teaching (even though they tried not to show it). . . . Little by little, we were becoming one big (slightly dysfunctional) family.

It wasn't long before a local sheriff's deputy figured out that most of the young criminals the department was looking for were at my gatherings on Tuesday and Thursday nights. Consequently, the sheriffs started showing up and making arrests in the gym. Of course, this really had a negative effect on my kids. Many of them were already terrified of cops. I got so mad that I finally went to meet the sheriff in person and explain the situation to him. He understood the positive impact we were having on the kids and on our county. He agreed to make the gym an asylum and to grant Tuesday and Thursday nights as arrest-free periods in Lewiston. (Otherwise, the sheriff's deputies would have been arresting our people on the way to or from our gym gatherings.)

The Rest of the Story

Weeks turned into months and months into years as we gathered kids at the gym, two nights a week, for five years. We won two community awards for our work with the kids, which inspired the Lions Club to sponsor us. Yet maybe the best thing that happened at the gatherings is that we met a thirteen-year-old boy named Gene, who became our fourth child through adoption.

But not everyone was happy with our work. Somewhere around the year-three mark, two Mormon missionaries dressed in slacks, white shirts and ties rode into the gym on their bikes. (We live in the mountains . . . they might as well have landed in a flying saucer.) In a loud, authoritative voice, one of them demanded to speak to the leader. One of the kids grabbed me and said, "Those creeps are asking for you."

"Hi, guys. What can I do for you?" I questioned.

"Are you the leader here?" one of them asked in an angry tone.

"Yep, what do you need?" I asked, with a hundred kids quickly gathering around.

"We're getting this place shut down! This is a government building, and you're using it for religious purposes," they proclaimed.

I don't think they understood the nature of the kids who were gathered there with us, or maybe they were just that clueless. Before I could answer, one of my tough kids said, "You better get the #%&*@! out of here before we beat your #*&!% and shove these bikes up your butts!"

Then the rest of the kids ran toward them, yelling and screaming threats. Both the Mormon men panicked and nearly fell off their bikes trying to get out of there. Truth is, they never returned!

Every gym night had a crisis. For instance, there was another incident in which a younger teenage boy was screaming at Kathy and calling her filthy names. He was mad because she had made him wait his turn to play a game. He continued yelling for several minutes, screaming at the top of his lungs like a crazy person. I finally went over to him and told him to leave. (The rule was, you screw up and you're out of the gym for one full week.) He refused to leave even after several requests, so I took him by the neck and ushered him out the door. He was resisting, of course, which made it harder to get him past the threshold.

About a half hour later, his mother showed up with the boy at her side and a bunch of neighbors in tow carrying rakes and shovels. They all demanded that I meet them outside. I went out, while at the same time trying to convince the other kids to stay in the gym. The boy's mother brought him over, showed me two red marks on his neck and asked, "Did you do this to my son?"

I have to admit that I must have been holding him tighter than I thought I was. "Yes, ma'am, it looks as if I did."

She went ballistic! Her neighbors began threatening me as I tried desperately to calm them all down. Finally, I just turned around and walked back into the gym, where I knew I was safe.

The woman shouted that I'd better not walk away from her, and her neighbors echoed her demand.

"If you would like to have a conversation with me, I'm glad to accommodate you, but I'm *not* going to let you intimidate me with your armed militia," I shouted in reply from inside the threshold of the gym doors.

The group out there finally calmed down, so I went back outside and told her my side of the story, while her neighbors stood there glaring at me.

She turned and yelled at her son this time, demanding to know if he had called my wife those dirty names and then refused to leave when I told him to go home.

The boy managed to squeal out a "*Yes . . .*"

"Get home!" she commanded. As he walked toward the street, she turned to me and apologized, and then kicked him in the butt not just once, but several times as they headed down the street toward their house.

I was just beginning to understand the level of abuse these kids were often exposed to. I had to find another method myself for removing the kids from the gym. I certainly couldn't call the police! A little side note: That young boy came back to the gym the next week, apologized to Kathy and spent the next five years honoring us. I also apologized to him for hurting him. It certainly wasn't my intent, and I never was mad at him. He turned out to be a great young man.

Broken Families Raise Broken Kids

About the third year of the gym gatherings, I decided to try a more holistic approach to helping all these kids become healthy. I wanted to start meeting with their parents to develop a plan for the well-being of their kids. I asked one of the kids, "Is it all right if I follow you home to meet with your folks?"

"I guess so," he replied reluctantly.

We walked down the street to his house, and the first thing I noticed was that his yard was littered with junk, the house windows were broken out, the door was wide open and dope smoke was pouring out of the doorway. My heart pounded with anxiety and sweat poured off my head as I neared the threshold. I hesitated for a minute, trying to reassure myself that it would be all right. I followed the boy inside to a dark, tiny front room. I stood there for a moment scoping out the space, trying to understand the scene unfolding in front of me. I observed that there was no furniture in the room except a mattress on the floor. The electricity was off in the house, and the place reeked of marijuana.

The boy introduced me to his mother, who was sitting on the floor in the corner of the front room, all drugged out. I somehow squeaked out a "*Hi,*" and then just turned around and walked back to the gym. I never talked to the young man about his mom again.

As time went on, I learned that only one of the more than 130 kids we ministered to even had a father at home (a good father, a bad father or any father at all in the house). In a surrogate way, Kathy and I became these kids' mom and dad. In most cases, we were the only healthy adults in their lives. Over the next few years, slowly our kids began to get whole, in spite of their broken homes. Many of the drug dealers got saved, and most of the kids began respecting themselves and started to embrace a sense of nobility, living lives that demonstrated honor, respect and character. We taught them how to have self-control and gave them tools to deal with their conflicts. Over time the fighting stopped, and the gym became a fun, peaceful, healthy environment full of laughter. (In chapter 6, I'll share more about our experience with the Lewiston girls.)

> In a surrogate way, Kathy and I became these kids' mom and dad. In most cases, we were the only healthy adults in their lives.

The Power of Compassion

Our influence on the hearts of the youth had a huge impact on everyone in the community. As our young people in Lewiston got healthy, crime plummeted, and the entire community was slowly transformed. People started taking more pride in their homes and yards, and even in their town.

In fact, if you drive through Lewiston now, you'll see a quaint mountain town. The homes are nicer, the yards are better kept, the gym is remodeled and there is a great ballpark that was once a field overgrown with weeds.

> The greatest miracle of all was taking place not in the kids around me, or even in the town we were in, but in the Kingdom within me.

Yet the greatest miracle of all was taking place not in the kids around me, or even in the town we were in, but in the Kingdom within me. Five years of wrestling with abandoned kids besieged with broken hearts, shattered dreams and wounded souls left an impression branded on my mind that would shape my worldview for decades. I spent many sleepless nights processing the fatherless nature of the world around me, wondering how to take the things I had learned in this tiny Lewiston community and apply them to the rest of the world.

To be honest, I wonder if the Lewiston experience mirrored in any way the challenges the nations of the world are facing today. What I have discovered in two decades of research is heart-wrenching . . . even shocking. In the following chapters, I will unfold what I have learned. *Be prepared* to be awakened to a world in serious trouble, and to the Kingdom with righteous solutions!

EPIC
TAKEAWAYS

- The gym and the Gospel: I had no idea what I had just said yes to!
- The ring story: Anyone can give away something expensive, but only those who understand sacrifice can give away something truly valuable.
- Five years "parenting" the tough kids: In a surrogate way, Kathy and I became these kids' mom and dad. In most cases, we were the only healthy adults in their lives.
- Every night a crisis, every year more whole: As our young people in Lewiston got healthy, crime plummeted, and the entire community was slowly transformed.
- The power of compassion: The greatest miracle of all was taking place not in the kids around me, or even in the town we were in, but in the Kingdom within me.
- *Be prepared*: The world is in serious trouble, but the Kingdom of God holds the righteous solutions!

TWO

Where Have All the Fathers Gone?

FORTY YEARS AGO, we moved from San Jose, California, to Lewiston because I was suffering from a nervous breakdown that lasted more than three years.[1] (It was ten years later that we opened the Lewiston gym for the probation kids.) In the midst of my misery, God spoke to me personally and gave me the following verses that would become the motto for my life and the core message for my legacy. In fact, these verses have played such a foundational role in my family's lineage that two of my adult grandkids have this Scripture reference tattooed on their bodies. (The tattoos were their idea, not mine. I don't have a single tat on my body.) Here's the passage:

> The Spirit of the Lord GOD is upon me, because the LORD has anointed me to bring good news to the afflicted; He has sent me to bind up the brokenhearted, to proclaim liberty to captives and freedom to prisoners; to proclaim the favorable year of the LORD and the day of vengeance of our God; to comfort all who mourn, to grant those who mourn in Zion, giving them a garland instead of ashes, the oil of gladness instead of mourning, the mantle of praise instead of a spirit of fainting. So they will be called oaks of righteousness, the planting of the LORD, that He may be glorified.

Then they will rebuild the ancient ruins, they will raise up the former devastations; and they will repair the ruined cities, the desolations of many generations.

Isaiah 61:1–4

God is taking the broken, the oppressed, the feeble, the captives and the prisoners and healing and commissioning them to rebuild the ruined cities of the world. This is the start, the inauguration and the commissioning of God to bring beauty from ashes!

It's been more than two decades since I last set foot in the Lewiston gym with those ragtag kids gathered around me. I often think back to those days with a fatherly fondness, wondering how relevant my experience in that tiny town of nine hundred people is to the challenges society is facing today in the megacities of America (and around the world). This book is the outgrowth of hundreds of hours of sleepless nights, praying for answers and researching the plight of millions of children with no daddies. In 2019, I was in a prayer gathering specifically centered around praying for our nation when I suddenly saw a vision of the prophet Malachi calling for the restoration of fatherhood and the return of fathers. Let me introduce you to Malachi. He lived somewhere around 2,500 years ago. He was an Israeli prophet who made a profound declaration that has never been so precisely placed as it is in this generation. He heard this from God:

> God is taking the broken, the oppressed, the feeble, the captives and the prisoners and healing and commissioning them to rebuild the ruined cities of the world.

Behold, I am going to send you Elijah the prophet before the coming of the great and terrible day of the LORD. He will restore the hearts of the fathers to their children and the hearts of the children to their fathers, so that I will not come and smite the land with a curse.

Malachi 4:5–6

Malachi perceived an epoch season when a generation would live in the absence of fatherhood . . . not simply the lack of fathers, but a famine of fathering. Let me explain. There have been many fatherless generations in the history of the world, caused most often by men dying in wars. For example, in 1860, when America's population was only 31 million people, 620,000 (mostly) men were killed in the Civil War. In fact, more American men died in that war than in all the other wars combined in the history of the United States! Fatherlessness reigned for more than two decades in America as our country made the slow recovery from that terrible war.

Yet in 1860, American fatherlessness was not a "heart" problem. The fathers were dead . . . their absence a side effect of war. Malachi's insights, although relevant to that generation and to every generation in one form or another, was specifically directed to a generation of *disheartened* fathers, sons and daughters. It's apparent to me that Malachi must have had us in mind, as we Americans and many others are living in the most fatherless generation ever experienced in modern times—and it has virtually nothing to do with the absence of fathers! In fact, there are more men alive today in the United States than ever before in our existence.

> We Americans and many others are living in the most fatherless generation ever experienced in modern times—and it has virtually nothing to do with the absence of fathers!

Welcome to the Revolution

So, what's the problem? I mean, why the fatherlessness? What's going on in the world that is having such an intensely negative impact on our families? That's the multibillion-dollar question! To answer this question accurately, we will have to journey back to the 1960s, when the foundation of fatherlessness was laid. The mantra of the sixties was sung by the then-famous band of Crosby, Stills, Nash & Young. In their song "Love the One You're

With," they basically chanted, "If you aren't with the person you love, it's okay, because you can have sex with the person you're with!"

The message of sixties songs was clear: "Free love" meant "make love" (so to speak) to anyone you're with, but make no commitments, no covenants . . . don't be loyal to anyone. Welcome to the sexual revolution! Did immorality begin in the sixties? No way! Immorality has been around since the beginning of time. But it was popularized in the sixties. For example, my mother got pregnant with me before she was married. It was 1954, just a few years before the sexual revolution began. As soon as my parents realized my mother was pregnant, they ran off and got married. Furthermore, when my grandfather found out my mother got pregnant before marriage, he disowned my mom and dad. (Thankfully, they worked it out a little while later.)

> ## Society once had moral standards, and consequently the culture itself helped people navigate their passions and sex drive.

Wow, your family must have been strong Christians because your grandparents and parents had strong moral convictions, you say.

No! They weren't even believers at the time, but they were Americans. People did sleep around back in those days, but they knew that what they were doing was wrong. Society once had moral standards, and consequently the culture itself helped people navigate their passions and sex drive.

All that went away in the sexual revolution. The shame and guilt of immorality was replaced with hippies, flower children, love, sex and rock and roll! It all climaxed at the close of the decade in a "music festival" called Woodstock that took place in August 1969 in Bethel, New York. There, 400,000 people gathered to party, take drugs and have sex in an open field. Woodstock was the icon of the proverbial sexual revolution, which thrust the decisive spear into the heart of American innocence. Purity fell hard on the battlefield of "free love" and crawled into the foxhole of irrelevance, bloodied and beaten by hippies like the Beatles, the Rolling Stones and the Grateful Dead, bands that reshaped American culture.

Amid the sexual revolution, another powerful force was emerging in our country—Darwinism. Although Charles Darwin's theory of evolution had been around since the mid-1800s and was introduced to the American school system in 1920, it never gained a foothold in modern thinking until the sexual revolution. The sexual revolution created the perfect environment for Darwinism to emerge, because people were violating their own moral values and were looking for a way to avoid answering to God for the guilt they were experiencing. Charles Darwin gave the world the excuse it needed to live like hell and not answer to heaven.

Darwinism basically says that all life, including human life, evolved from the same source over billions of years. This argument created two important core transitions in our thinking. First, instead of teaching that we were created in the image of God, as people once commonly believed, Darwinism taught that our ancestors were not divine, but apelike. This reduced the value society had for human life, because we then redefined humans as smart apes, and we elevated the animal kingdom to the worth of humans. Humans have hunted animals throughout most of history, so it is easy to see how this value system affected the way we viewed and treated our own kind. Consequently, now we protect animals and kill human babies in the womb!

Second, the theory of evolution taught us that we came about through a series of cosmic accidents that transpired over billions of years. This suggests that there was no divine design, no purpose for which we humans came about, and no Creator who loved us enough to die for us. Instead, it's just us—all alone on this giant rock we call Earth. This theory tells us that we are born to die with no eternity before us and no heaven after us. Such a philosophy naturally elevates pleasure as the highest goal of life on this "godforsaken" planet. *Eat, drink and be merry, for tomorrow we die* is the motto of Darwinism. Whether we agree with Darwin or not isn't as important as understanding that his "scientific" theories have led us to cultural mindsets that have ultimately been destructive to human dignity and morality.

What's the Outcome?

The sexual revolution and Darwinism are literally destroying the family unit in America, and everywhere else, for that matter! The social statistics

35

are so incredibly shocking that I actually had to check several sources to believe any of them.[2] Here is a brief overview: In 1950, less than 5 percent of all children were born out of wedlock in America. By 2017, that number rose by more than 1,700 percent![3] Today, about 71 percent of all black children and more than 50 percent of all Hispanic children are born out of wedlock; the number of whites and those of other races born out of wedlock has also risen exponentially, to nearly 40 percent.[4] Furthermore, estimates suggest that about 39 percent of all children in America will have a mother who is in a cohabiting relationship.[5] The African American community is suffering the most since 54 percent of their children are living with a single parent.[6] Globally, the specific numbers are different, but in many countries the trend toward fatherlessness is the same.

Maybe you are thinking, *Wow, Kris, these are alarming statistics, but what's that have to do with me since I am happily married, with healthy children, living the good life?*

I am glad you asked that question. Let me answer it with a story. About ten years ago, Danny Silk and I gathered approximately fifty community leaders in a room to talk about the most pressing issues that were plaguing Shasta County. We had leaders from nearly every sector of society there, including the police chief, the sheriff, the head of probation, the fire chief, a court judge, the superintendent of schools, several members of our city council, the mayor, many prominent businesspeople and a few public school teachers. We opened the meeting by going around the room and asking each person his or her perspective on what was at the root of our city's most serious problems. When the night was over and everyone had spoken, there was just one word on the whiteboard: *Fatherlessness!*

> **When the night was over and everyone had spoken, there was just one word on the whiteboard: Fatherlessness!**

Can you imagine our utter surprise when we discovered that the most experienced leaders in our community *all* came to the same conclusion? Not even the police chief or sheriff mentioned drugs, violence or the lack of funding for their departments as the root issue. It's so hard to capture in writing what happened to all of us that night as we just sort of sat there staring at each other, stunned. We were like a team of scientists who had suddenly stumbled upon the huge need for a cure for cancer, and yet we really had no cure . . . no magic pill . . . no real answers. Nearly a decade has passed since that fateful meeting, and very little has improved in our city. I guess it's one thing to understand the problem and quite another to find the cure.

Storm Clouds

Our American (and global) situation reminds me of Israel about 850 years before Christ. Israel was in deep trouble (again) as a man named Ahab became king and then married a demonized woman named Jezebel. Together, they carried Israel deep into the bowels of Baal worship, with the people sacrificing their babies on Baal's altar to satisfy this false god's need for blood. Much like abortion in our day, women threw their children on the altars of Baal without any resistance because he promised them pleasure and prosperity. The situation looked bleak as all Israel followed Baal. Resisting Ahab and Jezebel's edicts meant sure death for the Israelites.

Just when it looked as though all hope was lost, an obscure prophet emerged on the scene. His name was Elijah, and the guy had two things going for him: He had guts, and he knew God! Like a scene right out of an Arnold Schwarzenegger movie, Elijah commanded the clouds to stop raining, and suddenly it was "game on" with the wicked king and queen. It didn't rain a drop of water for three and a half years. In fact, the famine became so severe and food so scarce that the Israelites began eating one another!

Naturally, Elijah became public enemy number one as he traversed the wilderness and was supernaturally fed by ravens, and later by a widow who had no food herself. It's a wild story that climaxed with a showdown with Jezebel's 450 prophets of Baal at Mount Carmel. You can read it for yourself in 1 Kings 18, but let me recap it here for you. The Israelites all gathered there to watch their 450 politically correct prophets challenge one prophet of God. Outnumbered and outgunned, Elijah watched as Baal's prophets ranted and raved around their altar, trying to get their god to answer by fire. They cut themselves with knives and acted like a bunch of crazy people deep into the night. Of course, Elijah couldn't leave them alone. He taunted them all day long, shouting, "Maybe your god is on vacation, or maybe he's in the crapper!"

Nothing happened for Baal's brood of prophets. I mean, not even a little flicker or flame. Then it was Elijah's turn. He gathered the multitude close to him and poured gallons of water on his altar. Then he prayed a simple 30-second prayer, and *Bam!* God sent a supernatural firestorm from heaven that consumed the ox, the wood and the stones; it even licked up the water in the trench around the altar. (That's right; 1 Kings 18:38 says the fire "licked up the water.") The people rose up at Elijah's command and killed the 450 false prophets with swords in a feverish climax of righteous will. (I know, it's a little Old Testamentish.)

Next, Elijah journeyed to the top of Mount Carmel, knelt on the ground in the fetal position and began to pray for rain. While he prayed, he kept sending his servant to check his prayerful progress by looking for clouds in the sky. The servant returned six times with bad news . . . no clouds, no rain . . . no, no, no, no, no, no! But on the seventh time, something changed. A very small cloud formed, the size of a man's fist. This report stirred Elijah so profoundly that he jumped up and started running. He outran Ahab and his horse to Jezreel in the middle of a rainstorm (see 1 Kings 18:41–46). Ahab and Jezebel were soon overthrown, and Israel turned back to God. Elijah had singlehandedly turned the heart of a nation steeped in the occult back to God, in four short years!

Why am I telling you this story? Because the Lord is again sending Elijah the prophet in these last days, as the prophet Malachi announced so many years ago. The spirit of Elijah will turn the hearts of fathers back home . . . home to their daughters, home to their sons . . . *home!* In the same way that birds instinctively migrate south for the winter, there is coming an epic migration, a sort of supernatural awakening of fatherhood in the hearts of men. The drought of fatherhood has crested on the mountain of selfishness and isolation. That mountain is about to be washed away by a deluge of conviction and compassion—a mighty outpouring of God's Spirit. There is a cloud the size of a man's hand . . . get ready . . . it's about to rain. . . .

EPIC
TAKEAWAYS

- Beauty can come from ashes: God is taking the broken, the oppressed, the feeble, the captives and the prisoners and healing and commissioning them to rebuild the ruined cities of the world.
- Malachi's perception: There would come an epoch season when a generation would live in the absence of fatherhood . . . not simply the lack of fathers, but a famine of fathering.
- A national and global drought: We Americans and many others are living in the most fatherless generation ever experienced in modern times—and it has virtually nothing to do with the absence of fathers!
- The sexual revolution: Society's once-moral standards, which helped people navigate their passions and sex drive, all went away in the aftereffects of the sexual revolution.
- Man or monkey: Charles Darwin's theory of evolution gained a foothold during the sexual revolution, giving the world the excuse it needed to live like hell and not answer to heaven.
- Darwinism's "godforsaken" planet: This theory tells us we are born to die with no eternity before us and no heaven after us. Such a philosophy elevates pleasure as the highest goal of life on earth. This has led to cultural mindsets destructive to human dignity and morality.
- Elijah turned the tide: In his Old Testament day, this prophet dealt with Baal's evil influence on Israelite culture and turned the heart of a nation steeped in the occult back to God, in just four short years!
- The spirit of Elijah returns: In our day, the outlook may seem bleak, but there are storm clouds on the horizon! The drought of fatherhood is about to be washed away by a deluge of conviction and compassion—a mighty outpouring of God's Spirit.

THREE

Living in a Feminized Society

BEFORE WE DISCUSS THE POWERFUL RAMIFICATIONS of Malachi's outpouring and the restoration of the family, I want to take you on a journey in the next few chapters to expose you to a world in disarray, with society lurking through the long historic hallways of broken relationships, shattered dreams and deconstructed families. Like Nehemiah, who rose in the night to inspect the broken-down walls of Jerusalem so that he could develop a strategic plan for the reconstruction of his city, I want us, together, to understand how the foundations of our society have crumbled. My goal is that we would become cultural architects who know how to restore ruined cities and ultimately raise fathers of nations.

First, let's take a deep dive into fatherlessness. Fatherlessness has caused so many issues in our society that it's hard even to know where to start the conversation. What happens when fathers are absent from the lives of sons and daughters? What are the side effects of boys being raised exclusively by their mothers, or of girls having no daddy? Let's jump into the middle of this mess and see if we can unravel it. The fear of stereotypes has created a culture absent of masculine and feminine role models, all while the politically correct spirit moves us toward a genderless society. This dynamic has created the perfect storm, and a large portion of society has become rudderless, directed by the cultural currents of deception and confusion. This results in the false narrative of humanism (or worse), and it is not a manifestation of our Creator!

Contrary to popular opinion, men and women are *not* the same. It's important to understand the way God created humankind, so we can wrap our brains around His divine design. Here is the biblical account of the creation of the first woman:

> So the LORD God caused a deep sleep to fall upon the man, and he slept; then He took one of his ribs and closed up the flesh at that place. The LORD God fashioned into a woman the rib which He had taken from the man, and brought her to the man. The man said,
> "This is now bone of my bones, and flesh of my flesh; she shall be called Woman, because she was taken out of Man."
>
> Genesis 2:21–23

Did you notice that God took the woman "out of Man"? God put Adam to sleep, and then He literally took the *SHE* out of the *HE*. This means that the woman must have been in the man, or God could not have taken her out of him. God "separated" the image of Himself into two distinct persons—man and woman. All the attributes of womanhood were removed from the man when God literally took Adam and broke him in half.

The fear of stereotypes has created a culture absent of masculine and feminine role models, all while the politically correct spirit moves us toward a genderless society.

A few verses earlier, the Bible says that God decided it wasn't good for Adam to be alone, so He wanted to make a *suitable helper* for him (see Genesis 2:18). The Hebrew word for *suitable* is *neged*, and it means corresponding to, or opposite of.[1] The Hebrew word for *helper* is *ezer*, and it is used about nineteen times in the Old Testament: twice to describe a wife, and seventeen times to describe God Himself. Here are a couple of examples: "Our help [*ezer*] is in the name of the LORD, who made heaven and earth" (Psalm 124:8).

"How blessed is he whose help [*ezer*] is the God of Jacob, whose hope is in the LORD his God" (Psalm 146:5). These definitions assist us in understanding the place that God originally intended for a wife to have in her husband's life, and the way she would relate to him.

I should make it clear that I am not saying a man's wife should be a god to him, of course. I'm simply trying to point out that as men are incomplete without God because they were designed to be completed by Him, so also men and women are incomplete without each other. Please do not misunderstand me on this, either. I am not saying a man is incomplete unless he has a wife, or a woman is incomplete without a husband. Although I am a huge fan of marriage, as we will discuss in a moment, I am speaking to the bigger-picture truth that whether you are married or not, men and women need each other. And in order to be healthy and whole, society needs the gift that each gender brings to the world.

It is common for people to tell a guy that he needs to get in touch with his *feminine side*, yet the woman was taken *out* of the man—the feminine characteristics were removed from his *side*. The only way for a man to get in touch with his feminine side is to marry. Marriage merges the two so that they reemerge as one again. This holy union gives a husband access to his wife's strengths, and vice versa.

Triune Attributes

When God creates physical distinctions, He also fashions attributes that synergistically enhance the strength of those characteristics. For example, God didn't just give women breasts so they could physically feed their infants; He also planted a *nurturing* characteristic in their personhood. In other words, a woman's physical capability to breastfeed is a manifestation of her God-given ability and assignment as a *nurturer*. God first determines our divine purpose and then designs us with all the characteristics it takes for us to apprehend our divine destiny successfully.

I love the way Lou Engle put it when he preached one time at our church: "God doesn't give a person a dream; instead, God has a dream and He wraps the person around it." But it's the apostle Paul who said it best: "For we are His workmanship, created in Christ Jesus for good works, which

God prepared beforehand so that we would walk in them" (Ephesians 2:10). In other words, God prepared our work, our assignment, before He created us. He then designed each of us (spirit, soul and body) in light of our personal mission, so that we are fully equipped to fulfill our divine purpose. Hence, if you are man, you don't just have a penis so you can procreate; you are called and equipped to be a father.

> God first determines our divine purpose and then designs us with all the characteristics it takes for us to apprehend our divine destiny successfully.

Now let's dive a little deeper into these gender distinctions and flesh this out. Men are physically stronger than women, and also faster. (Of course, women are physically capable of carrying and giving birth to babies, which men have no ability to do.) In the Olympics, for example, women are about 10 percent slower in speed events, and there is approximately a 15 percent difference in strength events. This is the reason the NBA, NFL, MLB, UFC and almost every other professional sport are not co-ed. Do you really think, for example, that an all-women NFL team would be competitive against an all-male team? No! But with men's superior strength comes the responsibility to *protect* society and *provide* for their families. If I heard someone breaking into our house, for instance, it wouldn't occur to me to wake up my wife and send her downstairs to check it out. It's a man's responsibility to protect his family physically.

Yet on the other hand, God did give women superior abilities in other areas, such as *negotiating*. God also infused women with the gift of *intuition*, which gives them a "sixth sense," so to speak. These distinctions cause women to navigate life differently than men. Think about it: How many wars have been caused by women? One historian told me that women have initiated two wars in the history of the world, but he couldn't remember who the women were or when the wars were fought. That illustrates my point! When guys have a disagreement with someone, they commonly want to fight about it. Our default seems to be the irrational idea that "if I can beat you up, then I'm right." Women haven't used that option in society because they were created to be *peacemakers* and *reconcilers*, not warriors. Moreover, women have carried every man and woman in their wombs, causing them to be prone to *compassion*, not confrontation.

Furthermore, the Bible says, "The LORD God took the man and put him into the garden of Eden to cultivate it and keep it" (Genesis 2:15). Men were created to be *cultivators*, and women were created to be *incubators*—woman are "womb-men." A husband is designed to cultivate the garden of his wife's heart, and she, in turn, is meant to incubate the seeds of life he plants in her soul. For example, a husband gives his wife sperm, and she incubates it and gives him a baby. He buys her a house, and she makes it a home. He brings home the bacon, and she makes it a meal. A husband speaks gracious words to his wife, and she incubates those words and gives him a song.

> A husband is designed to cultivate the garden of his wife's heart, and she in turn is meant to incubate the seeds of life he plants in her soul.

Let me make it clear again that I am not trying to stereotype the genders, nor am I trying to limit the scope of either gender's occupation or role. I am simply pointing out that the way men and women approach life can be quite different at times.

Now, let's be clear—it's both intellectually irresponsible and scientifically refutable to say that women are inferior to men. But it's equally irresponsible to refuse to acknowledge that men are better at some things and women are better at others, by divine design. Yet in most of today's world, it is politically incorrect to gender-profile people or in any way acknowledge any strengths, weaknesses or distinctions related to gender, outside the obvious anatomical reproductive differences.

I have no desire to force anyone into a mold, or to make you feel bad or dysfunctional because you have a passion, responsibility and/or call that is different from the way I have expressed gender distinctions here. I am aware that I am painting the world with a very broad brush to try to bring some clarity to this highly volatile subject. I am not saying that men and women can't play the same role; I am just pointing out that they will approach the same assignment differently because of *who* they are, by divine design.

Fatherless Boys

Now that we understand that men and women are equally powerful but distinctly different, let's investigate some of the side effects that fatherlessness has on boys and men. Probably one of the most devastating consequences of fatherless on boys is that they become feminized because their mothers are raising them by themselves. It's not that moms are trying to turn their sons into daughters; it's simply that we teach what we know, but we impart who we are. Jesus put it like this: "A disciple is not above his teacher, but everyone who is perfectly trained will be like his teacher" (Luke 6:40 NKJV). The goal of fathering and mothering isn't just teaching our children life skills (although that certainly is important); it's also essential that our children become like us.

I can already hear the groanings: *That's heresy, Kris! We want our kids to be like Jesus, not like us!* Well, let's look at the great apostle Paul's instruction on fathering. He wrote:

> If you were to have countless tutors in Christ, yet you would not have many fathers, for in Christ Jesus I became your father through the gospel. Therefore I exhort you, be imitators of me. For this reason I have sent to you Timothy, who is my beloved and faithful child in the Lord, and he will remind you of my ways which are in Christ, just as I teach everywhere in every church.
>
> 1 Corinthians 4:15–17

Paul adamantly asserts here that there is a difference between tutors (or teachers) and fathers. Tutors teach sons and daughters important life lessons, but fathers (and mothers) are to be imitated until their offspring become like them. The old adage "more is caught than taught" applies here. In fact, this adage is really the hallmark of fatherhood (and motherhood). Furthermore, masculinity is not only inherited in every male's DNA, but it is also nurtured and cultivated by boys emulating their fathers.

Offended Mothers

Another dynamic fueling this dysfunction in fatherless homes is the side effect of offended mothers. It's hard to be a mother raising children alone and not be offended, angry and/or bitter at the man who impregnated you and then left you alone. It's just human nature to have negative feelings toward the man who is not carrying out his responsibility for the children he helped bring into the world.

Unforgiveness, bitterness and offense are toxic attitudes that are difficult to inoculate your children from. Imagine for a moment a girl abandoned by her father and raised by a mother who spreads her offense toward men to her daughter. Now envision this daughter maturing to a place of womanhood, where she is now looking for love and ready for sex. She has at least three unhealthy experiences working against her ability to find holistic companionship. First, she hasn't witnessed a healthy husband-wife relationship, so she doesn't understand how the masculine and feminine natures find rhythm together. Second, her mother has issues with her dad, and maybe even with men in general, so at best this young woman is cautious about men, and at worst she is angry at them and/or afraid of them. Third, she has experienced the pain of abandonment and rejection by her father, so she tends to view men as unreliable, unhealthy and indifferent.

Do you think these unhealthy factors might play a role in this young woman's choice of companions, especially with society's acceptance of lesbianism? You bet it could!

Gender Confusion

The truth is, fatherlessness is causing an epidemic of gender confusion, which is perpetrating and accelerating homosexuality, bisexuality, transgenderism and more. Men are literally being trained out of their ability to *protect*, *provide* and *promote*. As we discussed earlier, men were designed and commissioned by God to be protectors. Yet it's very difficult for young men to grow into this divine role when they are being raised exclusively by their mothers, who are inherently negotiators and peacemakers.

Before we get too deep here, let me point out that boys very much need the influence of a mother's strength in their lives. That strength needs to be tempered, however, with a father's mentoring influence. Some in the gay community are trying to convince us that it's perfectly normal for children to have two mothers or two fathers. They believe that children don't need a mother and a father. This is an incredible lie, and it's trying to destroy an entire generation of children!

> Boys very much need the influence of a mother's strength in their lives. That strength needs to be tempered, however, with a father's mentoring influence.

Furthermore, this lie has become so embraced in our society that the new educational curriculum introduced into the California school system in 2019 has removed the pronouns *he* and *she* in favor of only using *us* and *them*. The schools are now teaching our children that their gender is fluid, a choice our kids make. This curriculum also teaches our children that their birth sex is not necessarily their gender, which is promoting sexual confusion even in our youngest children. You want to talk about screwing up your kids—facilitated by the public school system, we have just introduced the doctrine of mental illness into our children. Most sensible, thinking people know that this kind of gender confusion is a mental illness, but that's by no means the prevailing mindset of our current deceived and deceptive culture.

The Doctors Are Sick

To make matters worse, the American Psychological Association (APA) is now embracing transgenderism as a normal lifestyle. The APA is a strong proponent of medical interventions because they have never been able to successfully treat gender dysphoria. The arrogance of the APA is in their assumption that when clinical counseling fails, there is no intervention at all that can successfully bring resolution.

Promoting medical/surgical interventions, then, is a concession to the limitations of the professions of psychiatry and psychology. Instead of admitting this, however, the "experts" instead affirm the social identities of those who are living the LGBTQ lifestyles. When the professionals, who are supposed to help heal us, instead normalize our sickness, it feels as if the patients have taken over the psych ward! (To be clear, our Bethel Church movement has seen Jesus heal and deliver many people from gender dysphoria, so there is hope and healing available in God.)

Sadly, mental illness, which is at the root of transgenderism, is *not* being adequately treated. A great deal of self-harm is therefore occurring in the name of political correctness. Current studies indicate that transgender-identifying adults are nineteen times more likely to commit suicide *after* gender reassignment, and that 90 percent of individuals who commit suicide have a diagnosed mental disorder.[2]

This shouldn't surprise us. Just consider what a man goes through to try to transition into a "woman." He must submit to hormone treatments, but the estrogen causes him to experience decreased sexual desire and complications with erectile function. Many transitioning men even go so far as to have their penis and testicles removed. (I can't even imagine the long-term ramifications of such a radical surgery.) A surgical vagina can be created for a transitioning man, but it results in a wound that must be taken care of for the rest of his life. Then, after all this, he still can't change his physical characteristics such as height or hand and foot size. His beard doesn't go away either, so he will often seek laser hair removal. Laryngeal surgery can change the pitch of his voice, but it reduces his range. Consequently, he often enters speech therapy in an attempt to make his voice sound more feminine.

The Thrill of Defeat

Transgender women (men who have "become" women) are now insisting on competing against biological women in female sports. I'm telling you, mental illness has become so politically correct in our culture that nobody will dare take a stand against this senseless, irrational movement that is literally destroying our nation and others. Society is rotting from the inside out, and our daughters and sons are the victims of this cesspool of lies.

Think about your daughter missing out on a full-ride athletic scholarship to a prestigious university because a couple of guys in her high school aren't fast enough to compete on the boys' track team. They decide to "transition" into girls and run against your daughter on her team, eliminating her chances to compete for a scholarship. I am not saying this is the only motive people have for transitioning, or that it's even the major reason, since there are usually much deeper mental illness issues that surround these situations. But if you think this kind of sports travesty is hype or nonsense, do your research. You'll be floored.

Here are a few paragraphs a transgender "woman" named Andrea Long Chu wrote. I took these from her article "My New Vagina Won't Make Me Happy: And It Shouldn't Have To," which was published in the *New York Times*:

> I feel demonstrably worse since I started on hormones. One reason is that, absent the levees of the closet, years of repressed longing for the girlhood I never had have flooded my consciousness. I am a marshland of regret. Another reason is that I take estrogen—effectively, delayed-release sadness, a little aquamarine pill that more or less guarantees a good weep within six to eight hours.
>
> Like many of my trans friends, I've watched my dysphoria balloon since I began transition. I now feel very strongly about the length of my index fingers—enough that I will sometimes shyly unthread my hand from my girlfriend's as we walk down the street. When she tells me I'm beautiful, I resent it. I've been outside. I know what beautiful looks like. Don't patronize me.
>
> I was not suicidal before hormones. Now I often am.
>
> I won't go through with it, probably. Killing is icky. I tell you this not because I'm cruising for sympathy but to prepare you for what I'm telling you now: I still want this, all of it. I want the tears; I want the pain. Transition doesn't have to make me happy for me to want it. Left to their own devices, people will rarely pursue what makes them feel good in the long term. Desire and happiness are independent agents.[3]

This article breaks my heart! We must tap into divine compassion for those who are so desperate to find healing and wholeness in their lives. Unfortunately, many Christians lead with truth absent of compassion, which tends to force transgender people deeper into their cave of isolation, loneliness and disillusion. Trans people need understanding, not judgment.

Feelings R Us

There is another unhealthy dimension to a feminized culture. It is not as radical as transgenderism, but it is more widespread. It is characterized by the word *authenticity*. *Authenticity* is being redefined as "being true to your feelings" instead of "being true to your purpose." This culture elevates feelings above facts and displaces science, logic and reason.

Feelings have become the proof test of truth. In other words, "If I feel it, it's true . . . how I feel is who I am . . . how I feel is how I am doing." This thought process goes so far as to say, "If I *feel* like a girl, I am a girl, even if I was born a boy."

> **The truth is that even though feelings are an important part of a healthy life, they are great servants and terrible masters.**

The truth is that even though feelings are an important part of a healthy life, they are great servants and terrible masters. It's common for people to have a strong opinion based on their feelings, and then to find "reasons" why they hold to that opinion. Eventually, someone comes along and dispels their "reasons" with facts, but they often don't change their minds, because their opinion was never really rooted in reason anyway. It was rooted in their emotions.

Hear Women Roar

In case you got the wrong impression in this chapter about the value I place on women, let me help you understand that I believe in powerful women. Not only did I write a book dedicated to empowering women, titled *Fashioned to Reign* (Chosen, 2013), but I also have two strong daughters, a beautiful daughter-in-law, four granddaughters and a powerful wife. I have been married for 47 years to my wife, Kathy, and although we have been through a lot together, we have always had a great marriage.

I do have to say that I believe Kathy was born about a hundred years too late, as she loves the rugged outdoors. Kathy likes horses (she has two of them), and she is an avid hunter and fisherwoman. I mean, the girl drives a four-wheel drive Dodge truck! As for me, although we lived in the Trinity Alps for twenty years, way back in the woods, I never enjoyed hunting or fishing. Yet Kathy is an amazing hunter. In 2019, she went on a hunting trip to Texas with my son Jason and my granddaughter Rilie, while I stayed home with her horses. Kathy killed a six-point buck with one shot, and a bobcat on the run with one bullet (in Texas, there is a bounty on bobcats since they destroy flocks and herds). She also shot a turkey at 100 yards with a single bullet. Just yesterday, she went fly-fishing in Shasta Lake with Jason and caught 32 bass by herself. I mean, the woman is amazing!

Yet Kathy is not a tomboy or a she-man. She is a beautiful, kind, gentle, feminine woman who loves being a wife and mother. I love her, and I'm excited for her to live fully alive, a completely actualized woman. She is a great role model for our daughters and granddaughters, who have always been empowered to do all God has called them to do. My oldest daughter, Jaime, co-pastors a church with her husband, Marty. My younger daughter, Shannon, is the principal and superintendent of an elementary school district.

The women in our family aren't reduced by stereotypes or oppressed by religious mindsets. They are great examples of women who have embraced their divine call as free women, empowered by God to be fully alive and to stand alongside men as leaders, mothers and matriarchs. Yet it's imperative to understand that even healthy, powerful women can't take the place of fathers in the lives of our children, because women are assigned by our Creator a distinct and different role than men in society and family. The same is true of men; they can't and never will fill the divine call of motherhood in the lives of their children, as hard as they may try. We therefore must restore the family unit back to its sacred trust, and we must stop the moral freefall that is plaguing our world today. Please join me in the fray as we shift the course of world history back to God and family.

EPIC
TAKEAWAYS

- The perfect storm: The fear of stereotypes has created a culture absent of masculine and feminine role models, all while the politically correct spirit moves us toward a genderless society.

- Contrary to popular opinion: Men and women need each other. And in order to be healthy and whole, society needs the gift that each gender brings to the world.

- Fashioned by God: He designed each of us (spirit, soul and body) in light of our personal mission so that we are fully equipped to fulfill our divine purpose.

- Different approaches to life: I'm not saying that men and women can't play the same role; I'm just pointing out that they will approach the same assignment differently because of *who* they are, by divine design.

- Fatherless boys: Boys become feminized because their mothers are raising them by themselves. It's not that moms are trying to turn their sons into daughters; it's simply that we teach what we know, but we impart who we are.

- Fatherless girls: At best, these young women are cautious about men, and at worst they are angry at men and/or afraid of them. This makes establishing a holistic relationship with a husband extremely difficult for them.

- Learning the lie: The schools are now teaching our children that their gender is fluid, a choice our kids make. And that their birth sex is not necessarily their gender, a lie that is promoting sexual confusion even in our youngest children.

- Gender dysphoria: Medical professionals once saw gender confusion as mental illness (and those with a Christian worldview still see it that way). Most of today's medical "experts," however, see gender confusion as normal and propose surgical/medical intervention or no intervention at all.

- Tap into divine compassion: Many Christians lead with truth absent of compassion, which tends to force transgender people deeper into their cave of isolation, loneliness and disillusion. Trans people need understanding, not judgment!
- Feelings R Us: Today, feelings have become the proof test of truth. *Authenticity* is being redefined as "being true to your feelings" instead of "being true to your purpose." This culture elevates feelings above facts and displaces science, logic and reason.
- Restoring the family unit: Even healthy, powerful women can't take the place of fathers in their children's lives, because our Creator assigned women a distinct and different role than men in society and family. The same is true of men; they can't fill the divine call of motherhood in the lives of their children.

FOUR

Toxic Masculinity?

I LOVE WATCHING THE WOMEN IN OUR FAMILY LIVE OUT their feminine identity, fully actualized, free from the politically correct spirit, celebrated as daughters of the King and empowered to fulfill their God-given destiny. I want men to have the same freedom—men being men, their masculinity celebrated, empowered and embraced in society. But there's a term that's threatening the very nature of men and shaming their God-given identity—the term *toxic masculinity*.

Toxic masculinity is a phrase that has been around since the eighties, but it has gained a lot of traction and redefinition in the last few years. It's now defined by the idea that masculinity is itself toxic. Here is the Wikipedia definition (I am using the Wikipedia definition purposefully, not because it's the most accurate definition, but because it's the definition most influenced by our current culture):

> The concept of toxic masculinity is used in academic and media discussions of masculinity to refer to certain cultural norms that are associated with harm to society and men themselves. Traditional stereotypes of men as socially dominant, along with related traits such misogyny and homophobia, can be considered "toxic" due in part to their promotion of violence, including sexual assault and domestic violence. The socialization of boys in patriarchal societies often normalizes violence, such as in the saying "boys will be boys" about bullying and aggression.[1]

I am not sure if you caught the key buzzwords scattered throughout that definition—words like *traditional*, *homophobia*, *socially dominant*, *patriarchal societies* and *aggression*. Let's be clear about what is being proclaimed here: If you are a male and you believe that homosexuality is wrong, immoral, unnatural and/or a sin, then you are a toxic man. If you are a male with "traditional values," you are toxic. If you are a male who is "socially dominant," "aggressive" and/or "patriarchal," then you are toxic.

> The answer to these toxic cultures is healthy fathers, role models and mentors who teach men how to manage their masculine attributes toward wholeness and nobility.

Do you notice any theme here? The very nature of manhood is being shamed and redefined to emasculate men and make them more feminine. *Why?* you ask. Because the LGBTQ movement wants men and women to be interchangeable, as I pointed out earlier. They want to deconstruct the traditional family, with the goal of normalizing gay marriage and having it be seen as natural for children to be raised by two dads or two moms.

Let me be clear—I am not saying that certain male attributes like aggression, left unchecked or untrained, are okay. As a matter of fact, they are not. They lead to bullying, violence, strife and contention, which produce toxic cultures in our homes, schools and communities. Yet the answer to these toxic cultures is healthy fathers, role models and mentors who teach men how to manage their masculine attributes toward wholeness and nobility.

Dr. Abilash Gopal, a psychiatrist educated at Princeton, Tufts, Harvard and UCSF who has a therapy practice in San Francisco, writes this in his blog post "Reviving Romeo: Reclaiming the male identity in the age of 'toxic masculinity'":

> Masculinity is under attack. If you haven't noticed, then you've been living under a rock. By now, you've probably heard that the American Psychological Association has joined the fray by reframing masculinity as a mental illness. The APA claims that "traditional masculinity—marked by stoicism,

competitiveness, dominance, and aggression—is, on the whole, harmful." Who's to blame for corrupting innocent boys with these toxic urges? According to the APA, it's the patriarchy. So men are to blame for ruining men.[2]

Did you notice that the American Psychological Association, which normalized transgenderism, is the same organization that is diagnosing *masculinity* as a mental illness?! Any idea who has taken over control of the APA?

The truth is, healthy masculinity is essential to building healthy communities. Yet these days, men are being socially castrated to reduce their influence in society and thus silence their voices. The truth is, it's the lack of fathering that is at the root of the rising violence among men.

There's an Elephant in the Room

Let me share a story with you that will help us understand the important role that fathers play in creating healthy cultures.[3] Years ago, Kruger National Park in South Africa faced an elephant of a problem—literally, as the African elephants, once at risk of becoming extinct, bred so well in the park that their sheer numbers became unsustainable. The park rangers therefore devised a plan to transplant some of the African elephants to Pilanesberg National Park, also in South Africa, to thin the herds.

The main challenge they faced was how to transport such huge animals to another game reserve, as you can't really FedEx an elephant! Finally, one of the rangers came up with the idea of building special harnesses to airlift the elephants to the other park with helicopters. (When birds poop on our car windshield, we always say, "Aren't you glad elephants can't fly?" So this story roused a ton of laughter in me as I envisioned the possibilities!) The helicopter idea worked great, except that the harnesses broke when they tried to transport the full-grown male elephants. These bulls were just too heavy for the harnesses. (Gosh, I hope they figured that out before the helicopter got very high off the ground!) The rangers made the decision to keep the larger, mature male elephants at Kruger and only transport some of the females and young male elephants to Pilanesberg.

This is where the plot thickens! Sometime after the elephant relocation project was complete, the rangers at Pilanesberg began to discover an unusual, somewhat startling problem. They began finding the dead bodies of endangered white rhinoceroses all around the reserve. The rangers first suspected poachers, as white rhino horns are so highly valued on the black market. But there were no bullet holes in the animals, and their valuable horns were left intact. A deeper investigation revealed that the white rhinos had been killed violently, suffering deep puncture wounds on their bodies. The investigative team, still bewildered by the problem, set up hidden cameras around the park to try to capture the villains on video.

What the rangers caught on camera was shocking, to say the least. The young male elephants that had been relocated to the park had become a violent and aggressive predatory gang, terrorizing all the other animals in the reserve. In fact, the young elephants were caught on camera chasing down the rhinos, knocking them over and stomping and goring them to death with their tusks. This was previously unheard of since elephants and rhinoceroses had cohabited for centuries.

The rangers developed a theory to explain the situation. Juvenile male elephants experience what's called *musth*, a state of frenzy triggered by increases in testosterone and the mating season. Normally, dominant bulls control this testosterone-induced frenzy in the younger males and keep it in check. But the rangers theorized that, left without the elephant modeling of more mature bulls, these younger elephant menaces were missing the civilizing influence of their elders that nature intended them to have.

To test the theory, the rangers constructed a bigger, stronger harness and used it to fly in some of the older bulls that had been left behind at Kruger. In a matter of weeks, the bizarre, violent behavior of the juveniles stopped completely. The older bulls taught them that their murderous behaviors were not elephant-like at all. Soon, these once-delinquent and dangerous younger elephants were following the older, more dominant bulls around and learning how to follow pachyderm protocol and become the elephants they were meant to be.

What an incredibly intriguing story, which begs the question of how the absence of human fatherhood in our twenty-first-century culture is affecting masculine aggression, hostility and violence. To get a clear picture of the effects of fatherlessness on American culture, let's take a look at some relevant statistics and try to ascertain the story that emerges from them. First of all, it's important to understand that 90 percent of all American inmates in prison are men, not women (note that this is also true in most other countries).[4] What is even more revealing is that 75 to 90 percent of all of these inmates grew up without a father![5] (Just a note here: Various studies have come to slightly different statistical conclusions on father-less among inmates, thus the variance you will find on this statistic. My guess is that differing definitions of "fatherlessness" affect the statistical outcomes.)

Wait Till . . .

The statistics in America and other nations paint a grim picture of the plight of the fatherless and the terrible effect fatherlessness is having on society. What is it about having a dad that helps boys become more peaceful men? I think the answer is pretty simple, and most of us instinctively know what it is. Before I give you the answer, however, finish this sentence for me: A mom says to her misbehaving son, "*Wait till . . .*"

I've posed this question to several gatherings of thousands, in many different countries, and in *every* instance (and without hesitation) the audience will shout back, ". . . *your father gets home!*"

That's right! One of the most important roles of fatherhood is discipline. Of course, mothers must also be part of disciplining children, but it's the dads who are equipped and commissioned to lead in this area of parenting. Consequently, the absence of fatherhood can create behavioral tolerance and a lack of self-restraint. Much like the young male elephants that became violent when the adult bull elephants were removed

> **One of the most important roles of fatherhood is discipline. Of course, mothers must also be part of disciplining children, but it's the dads who are equipped and commissioned to lead in this area of parenting.**

from the herd, violence increases exponentially when human fathers are absent from their families.

The author of the book of Hebrews gave us profound insight into this topic. He wrote,

> It is for discipline that you endure; God deals with you as with sons; for what son is there whom his father does not discipline? But if you are without discipline, of which all have become partakers, then you are illegitimate children [bastards] and not sons. Furthermore, we had earthly fathers to discipline us, and we respected them; shall we not much rather be subject to the Father of spirits, and live? For they disciplined us for a short time as seemed best to them, but He disciplines us for our good, so that we may share His holiness. All discipline for the moment seems not to be joyful, but sorrowful; yet to those who have been trained by it, afterwards it yields the peaceful fruit of righteousness.
>
> Hebrews 12:7–11

Several exciting and clarifying facts bleed through this passage. First, the author assigns discipline to fathers as part of their God-given role in the life of their sons. In fact, he says discipline is a sign or manifestation of the legitimacy of sonship in the life of a child. Yet another way to look at this passage is that children born out of wedlock, who live without a father, are not disciplined in this way by a dad and therefore can struggle to develop noble character. Thankfully, the writer reassures us that God's fathering in our lives transcends that of our earthly fathers, which thus gives us hope of maturing in the Lord even if we grow up fatherless.

Another thing that stands out from this passage is that discipline is not so much an action as it is a culture, a way of training children. Furthermore, the good fruit of noble character developed through discipline is often preceded by some tough intervals of repeated disobedience. This is why consistency is so important in the lives of children. Discipline must be predictable to be effective. I remember being at home one night, listening to Kathy try to get the kids to stay in their beds and go to sleep. She was in the middle of a project, while I was on a long-distance phone call, so disciplining the kids that night was a big inconvenience. I could hear the kids upstairs laughing and playing. Finally, Kathy yelled, *"Get in bed and go to sleep—now!"*

A few minutes later, quiet giggles descended again from upstairs, so in a more demanding voice Kathy shouted, "*Get in bed now! Do you hear me? Or I'm going to come up there and spank all three of you!*"

The silence was short-lived, and soon the kids were back at it again. This time, Kathy walked to the staircase as if she were going upstairs and shouted, "*Did you hear me? I said get in bed and go to sleep. I'm coming up there and I'm going to spank all of you. Now get in bed! NOW! Get in bed!*"

Not ten minutes passed before the party began again. Livid, Kathy began her rant again: "*GET into BED!*"

I interrupted her tirade with a laugh, mocking her with, "*I'm going to spank you. . . . Do you hear me? I mean it! I'm not lying! I'm coming up there! Do you hear me? NOW! I said NOW!*"

She looked over at me with a smile and said, "Shut up!" Then she marched upstairs and took care of business. Later that evening, we talked deep into the night about changing the way we disciplined our kids. We agreed to give our children one warning and then act. We spent the rest of that year encouraging each other to be consistent, predictable and persistent. Soon, reliable parenting became our culture, our rhythm and our way of life. The results were slow but remarkable. Our home was transformed into a place of peace, and over time our children learned to listen and be respectful.

While we're on the subject of respect, I want to make it clear that it's important for husbands and wives to take a noble stand for one another with their children. For instance, whenever one of our children (most commonly in their teenage years) was disrespectful to Kathy, I felt it was my duty as her husband and my responsibility as their father to defend her honor. I would say something like, "You're talking to my wife. You always have permission to express your opinion in this house, but you will not disrespect my wife! Go clean up your mess with her and change your attitude." Kathy would do the same thing for me so we could demonstrate to our kids that husbands and wives defend one another's honor.

Ready, Set, Go

Another important lesson Kathy and I learned in those days is that we teach our children *when* we are going to act. Consequently, they wait for our action signal before they behave. We often think it's the *type* of signal we send that inspires them to action, and we don't understand that it's the fact that *we act* after our action signal that motivates them. The most common example parents cite of this is yelling. So many moms and dads complain that their children don't obey them until they yell. The truth is that yelling is your action signal.

Let me illustrate it like this: Your two-year-old is touching the buttons on the TV. You tell him, "Johnny, don't touch the TV." He looks over at you and defiantly pokes a button. Now you lower your tone and raise your voice: "*Johnny*, I told you not to touch the television. Get away from there *now!*" He looks at you and then changes the channel. Now you've had it and yell, "*Johnny, get away from that TV right NOW!*" You've determined that if he touches it again, you're going to slap his hand or take definitive action—a kind of escalation that he has experienced before with you, so now he walks away. You think he obeyed you because you yelled, but he obeyed because you gave him your action signal. You yell right before you act, and Johnny knows there are no consequences for his actions until you shoot up that flare!

The other lesson Johnny learns from your yelling is that he only must obey you when you are mad. He doesn't therefore relate his obedience to his own bad actions; instead, he relates his obedience to your bad temper. When we yell at our kids, we move from parenting to being peers. The truth is that Johnny needs to learn how to respect authority and honor people who have power and/or influence over him. Someday, he will likely encounter someone who has authority over him and knows it. Maybe it will be a police officer who tells him to do something in a nice tone of voice. But Johnny isn't used to obeying authority; he is accustomed to waiting for the angry signal before he submits, and he therefore winds up in jail. I wonder how many young men are sitting in prison because they misread someone else's signal. Scary thought!

You want to stop yelling at your kids? It's simple. Speak softly and carry a big stick (hopefully, the stick is a metaphor). Give your children one warning and then act for their sake, not because you are mad. Remember, punishment says, "I will make you pay for what you did wrong to me." But discipline says, "I love you too much to leave you the way you are."

A Wise King Speaks

Consistent discipline is a ton of work, but it's paramount in the lives of children. I love the way King Solomon put it: "Foolishness is bound up in the heart of a child; the rod of discipline will remove it far from him" (Proverbs 22:15). Some parents have used verses like this to give themselves permission to punish their children or even abuse them in the name of discipline. The sad fact is that Child Protective Services (CPS) cites religious families as having some of the most abusive homes in our communities. This has caused many parents to avoid discipline altogether in order to evade even the appearance of abuse. This is an overreaction and a huge parenting mistake. We *must not* abuse our children, yet it's still true that discipline is the antidote for foolishness. The apostle Paul spoke into this balance beautifully when he said, "Fathers, do not provoke your children to anger, but bring them up in the discipline and instruction of the Lord" (Ephesians 6:4).

Solomon brought to light another profound truth—that foolishness is an attitude, not an action. In other words, it's imperative that we discipline attitudes long before attitudes become actions. In this way, children learn to manage their inner world, their emotions, their desires and their temptations before those ever become behaviors. But one of the challenges we face in the twenty-first century is that people never learned when they were growing up how to delay gratification or manage their appetites. The ultimate outcome of this is a culture

> **Discipline isn't happy hour, but it is essential in developing noble character in our kids.**

where people identify themselves by their feelings, passions and desires. So much of this could be solved if parents would just step up to the plate, stop being their kids' best friends and start becoming fathers and mothers. Discipline isn't happy hour, but it is essential in developing noble character in our kids.

I often cringe when I observe some of the things I see parents doing. The other day I was in a store where a poor, tired young mom was "shopping" with her two young kids. A girl who looked about four years old was walking next to her, while a two-year-old boy was "sitting" in the grocery cart. The child in the cart was screaming for ice cream while grabbing everything within reach off the shelves. This mom was obviously frazzled, and I felt sorry for her. But a few minutes into the younger child's rant, this mom did the unthinkable. She gave him the ice cream he was screaming for. At that moment, everything became very clear to me. That little boy was leading this family because he had figured out how to control his mother. She was happy to relegate her leadership to her little Caesar. She became his subject so he would stop punishing her.

What this mom probably doesn't realize is that she is growing a selfish, self-centered monster. Soon her boy will have a sex drive that he will satisfy by badgering some girl in the same way that he punished his mom into quenching his ice-cream passion. He is learning the ways of the world by believing the lie that he is designed for instant gratification and created to meet the endless and ever-changing desires of his feelings. This may seem harsh, but maybe it's the reason that most rapists have grown up in fatherless homes. According to the *Criminal Justice and Behavior* journal, 80 percent of all rapists, who often also have anger problems, grow up fatherless. That's fourteen times the national average of those who have fathers in America![6]

More Troubles

Not only are fatherless males dramatically more violent in society, but fatherlessness also has a profoundly negative effect on the rate of youth suicides. In fact, the U.S. Department of Health and Human Services, Bureau of the Census reported that 63 percent of all youth suicides involve kids from fatherless homes, which is five times the national average of those who have fathers.[7] The lack of discipline in fatherless homes can create a culture where there is no sense of closure for sin.

Let me explain. God created us with a justice nature like His own. In other words, we inherently believe that when someone does something wrong, there should be consequences for his or her offense. For instance, when we hear about a violent rape in which the perpetrator was released without any penalties (no jail time or even probation), we are livid. Why? Because we were created for closure that can only come through justice. In fact, our justice nature is the reason we find cop movies so entertaining. The first scene of every great cop movie is usually some reprobate committing a hideous crime. Now we are hooked. We feel compelled to watch the rest of the show because our soul needs closure. Hence we must see the criminal get what he deserves (usually at the end of the movie).

When there is a healthy father figure in the home and he inspires righteous discipline in the lives of his children, a culture of justice and closure is created.

The same dynamic is at work in our own soul when we violate our value system. For example, let's say we lie and don't get caught, or we get caught but receive no consequences for lying. Our internal justice nature requires us to have closure, yet we received no consequences for our violation. We therefore create our own sense of justice by punishing ourselves. Law enforcement agencies understand this principle. Criminals subconsciously want to get caught, so they inadvertently leave clues.

Self-hatred and self-destruction are most often rooted in injustice. On the other hand, when there is a healthy father figure in the home and he inspires righteous discipline in the lives of his children, a culture of justice and closure is created. This culture slams the door shut on self-hatred and self-destruction because the ecosystem of justice is complete, which brings closure to the hearts of the family.

The Three-Legged Stool

When we don't find connection, closure and protection in our homes, we often flee. This is the reason 90 percent of all homeless and runaway children are from fatherless families—a staggering 32 times the average![8]

Metaphorically speaking, like a three-legged stool, it takes a *mom*, a *dad* and a *child* to complete the stool of stability in life. A father without a mother or a mother without a father can result in a two-legged stool

> Metaphorically speaking, like a three-legged stool, it takes a *mom*, a *dad* and a *child* to complete the stool of stability in life.

home environment that can easily become unstable. In fact, according to the Centers for Disease Control and Prevention (CDC), 85 percent of all children who have serious behavior disorders were raised without a father, which is, again, a *staggering* 20 times the national average.[9]

It's no wonder that children are nine times more likely to drop out of high school if they grow up without a dad. In fact, according to the National Principals Association, 71 percent of all high school dropouts are fatherless.[10]

The statistics are staggering, yet society is blowing through the caution signs like a drunk driver with a death wish, and the last sign we blasted through read *CAUTION: Dead-End Road Ahead!* Our country is in serious trouble (as are many other countries facing this same issue), but much like the proverbial frog boiling to death, we've lost touch with what is—or should we say, with *who* is—in the dang pot. The bad news is that the problem is serious, yet the good news is that the solution is unquestionably simple: "Daddies, please go home!"

EPIC
TAKEAWAYS

- Toxic masculinity buzzwords: *traditional, homophobia, socially dominant, patriarchal societies* and *aggression.* Society now views all of these as toxic.

- Masculinity under attack: The very nature of manhood is being shamed and redefined to emasculate men and make them more feminine. Yet healthy masculinity is essential to building healthy communities.

- Elephant-sized issues: Like juvenile bull elephants going through *musth* without male mentors to temper their tempers, young men in society today badly need to experience the *"Wait till your father gets home!"* dynamic.

- A noble stand: Husbands and wives need to come together and defend each other's honor in front of children who need discipline.

- Action signals signal behavior: We often think it's the *type* of signal we send that inspires our kids to action, and we don't understand that it's the fact that *we act* after our action signal that motivates them.

- Solomon says: "Foolishness is bound up in the heart of a child; the rod of discipline will remove it far from him" (Proverbs 22:15). While that isn't a license for child abuse, consistent (and appropriate) discipline is paramount in the lives of children.

- Our inherent justice nature: God created us with a justice nature like His own. We inherently believe that when someone does something wrong, there should be consequences for his or her offense. We even apply this to ourselves and our behaviors.

- Rooted in injustice: Self-hatred and self-destruction are most often rooted in our sense of injustice when our own poor behaviors don't result in consequences. But the kind of culture that a healthy father figure inspires slams the door shut on self-hatred and self-destruction because the ecosystem of justice is complete within the family.

- Staggering statistics: My country of America and many other nations are in serious trouble due to the effects of fatherlessness, but the solution is simple: "Daddies, please go home!"

FIVE

The Rite of Passage

ONE OF THE MAIN FACTORS fueling the dynamic that some have termed *toxic masculinity* (which we discussed in the previous chapter) is a society absent of the rite of passage. It is the responsibility of healthy fathers to invite sons into manhood. In his book *Man Maker Project*, author Chris Bruno puts it like this: "Boys may be born of the womb, but men are born of *men*. It is a second birth—the birth borne of the masculine."[1]

God tasks fathers with the duty of preparing boys for manhood, which culminates with the *rite of passage*. The rite of passage in simple terms is the process in which men acknowledge that a boy has become a man. Some ethnic groups have *coming-of-age* rituals embedded into their culture that help formalize this epoch transition in a young person's life.

The Jewish community has the most well-known rite of passage, called the *Bar Mitzvah*. In this tradition, thirteen-year-old Jewish boys celebrate their Bar Mitzvahs by demonstrating their commitment to their faith and the maturity to follow Jewish law responsibly. Jewish boys often spend months learning and preparing for their Bar Mitzvahs.

Journey-less Men

When the journey to manhood is undermined by dysfunctional fathers or derailed by broken families, an important part of manhood becomes dormant in the life of a young man. The leadership characteristics inherent in men will remain asleep or latent, waiting to be awakened by a father. Thus, these boy/men who are without dads become players instead of leaders, elevating pleasure above purpose—largely because they are ill-equipped for manhood, and the fear of failing paralyzes them.

One thing this paralysis does is cause such boy/men to relate to women only as mothers and sisters, but not as wives and lovers. This is further exacerbated by the fact that fatherless men have never observed how a healthy husband relates to his wife. Consequently, these men don't pursue lovers; they pursue mothers. They are looking for a woman who will care for them, not a woman whom they can provide for, protect and promote.

Another consequence of this unnatural dynamic is boy/men who grow old but never seem to grow up. These men often shirk responsibility, elevate pleasure above purpose and hibernate in the proverbial cave of video games and porn sites. These men commonly concede that they feel like boys in a man's world, because they are ill prepared for real life in the jungle of reality. They are scared little boys dressed up in NO FEAR T-shirts and Superman tattoos. Their heroes are sports figures and pop artists . . . entertainers with millions of Twitter followers, but often without an ounce of character.

> **Overly mothered men tend to feel entitled. In fact, they are frequently obsessed with the idea that it's someone else's responsibility (usually the government) to take care of them.**

Overly mothered men tend to feel entitled. In fact, they are frequently obsessed with the idea that it's someone else's responsibility (usually the government's) to take care of them. Although many of them are highly educated, they are often still unprepared for the responsibility of having a family.

Case in Point

Here at Bethel Church, we have a school of ministry that has more than 2,500 full-time students. The school is filled with boy/men who are trying to navigate their way through life without being fully awakened to manhood. Although there are more than 1,100 beautiful single women from more than seventy countries around the world in the school, and they all love God, it's common for our male students to say, "I can't find a woman to marry!"

I tell them, "Men, looking for a woman in the school of ministry is like fishing at the hatchery. I mean, just throw out your line and the fish will bite. Heck, you don't even have to bait the hook in our environment."

Our female students ask us all the time if it's okay for them to pursue a man instead of waiting to be pursued. I tell them, "You were born to be pursued, adored and chased by noble men, but in these days of powerless, ill-prepared men, you might just have to jump in the boat because these guys just aren't fishing."

When I talk to a guy and suggest that he pursue a certain woman, the most common response I hear is, "I can't ask her out. She's like a sister to me."

The truth is that a lot of these men don't know how to relate to lovers, so they only view women as sisters or mothers. It truly greives me! I feel so bad for all these daughters who are awakened for love, but are living among boy/men who are asleep to manhood.

Blind Men

The truth is, we often question *what* we see, but we seldom question *how* we see. In other words, we tend to view the world through an "accent" we don't know we have, unless, metaphorically speaking, we encounter someone who has a different "accent." Otherwise, we remain *unconsciously ignorant*, meaning we don't know that we don't know.

What I am trying to say is that these boy/men honestly believe they can't find a lover, not realizing they wouldn't know one if she stood right in front of them. Subconsciously, they are filtering or vetting these godly, available women out. This is further compounded by the fact that we tend to make up excuses in our minds to explain our behavior to *ourselves*, to reassure us that the situation is not our fault.

> We tend to make up excuses in our minds to explain our behavior to *ourselves*, to reassure us that the situation is not our fault.

This dynamic is illustrated so well in Malcolm Gladwell's bestselling book *Blink: The Power of Thinking without Thinking*. In his book, Gladwell shares several intriguing stories about people who do some amazing things but are clueless as to why they do them. For instance, he tells the story of a famous baseball player named Ted Williams. Ted was one of the greatest hitters of all time. When people asked him how he managed to bat so well, he explained to them that he "could look the ball onto the bat." But the crazy thing is that when they studied batting habits with the aid of high-speed cameras, they found that human beings couldn't track a ball onto a bat because it's only a three-millisecond event. Ted's explanation did not match his actions. Was Ted lying? No! In the absence of a logical explanation, his mind had created a justification to put the question to rest.[2]

In the same way, these boy/men honestly believe that although they live in the midst of 7.5 billion people on the planet—which means there are more people alive today than in all of previous history *combined*, and half of those are women—they literally can't find a wife. It's *unbelievable*!

Not the Marrying Kind

All of this adds up to men who lack confidence in their ability to lead and provide for a family because it has never been modeled for them. They therefore delay marriage or reject it altogether, often choosing to cohabit rather than make a marriage covenant.

These guys tend to gravitate toward a cohabiting arrangement because it feels more like being friends with benefits than like being a husband with the responsibility of a family. Of course, this feeds the ecosystem of fatherlessness, as many of these cohabiting women become impregnated by these boy/men, who are most often then driven away by the responsibility of fatherhood. Some women caught in the narrative of uncommitted guys get pregnant on purpose, thinking it will awaken the fathering instinct in their boyfriends. They refuse to understand that their guy is literally a *boy*-friend, not a father.

Although both boy/men and fathers have a penis, the resemblance pretty much ends at their sperm count. These are impostors, pretend men masquerading as grown-ups with tough talk and manly muscles. But they are unmasked through obligation, deflated by duty and uncovered with the accountability of a covenant.

Let me be clear—I am not saying that these guys are bad men, cruel or corrupt. I am simply pointing out that the process of manhood has been derailed in their lives. The natural progression of their maturity has suffered the harsh reality of suspended development. These guys are like ships left to drift in the ocean of humanity, without the rudder of fatherhood to guide them. Spiritual men must become surrogate dads who care and who board these lost ships and guide them to the harbor of maturity.

The Peter Pan Syndrome

In *Man Maker Project*, Chris Bruno unearths what is referred to as the *Peter Pan Syndrome*, which gives us deeper insight into the psyche of a fatherless male. Bruno describes the condition as the refusal to grow up and says this:

> This refusal to grow up finds its archetype in the famous Peter Pan, who says to Wendy, "No one is going to catch me, lady, and make me a man. I want always to be a little boy and have fun." It is far easier and more comfortable to deny passage than to face it. Without the active intervention of a father (or another older man) to take the boy out, he will remain stuck in childhood indefinitely. The Peter Pan man remains consumed by his own self-centeredness and cannot break free of his mother's influence. Even if she pushes him from the nest, he remains trapped in the Neverland of unending childhood. Something must be done, and it is up to the father to do it.[3]

> **It is much more common to meet "Peter Pan" on the streets of America than it is to meet "Rambo," the macho man.**

Bruno went on to say that men struggling with the Peter Pan Syndrome cannot face their adult sensations and responsibilities, and that social and professional relationships are difficult for them because of their irresponsibility and narcissism.

I think Chris Bruno hit the proverbial nail on the head. In fact, I would propose that we are in the midst of a "Peter Pan culture," in that this syndrome has become the norm in society. It is much more common to meet "Peter Pan" on the streets of America than it is to meet "Rambo," the macho man. Now, let me be clear—neither of these syndromes is healthy. But "Rambo," or maybe more accurately the "Marlboro Man" dynamic, was the pinnacle of the manly mandate in most communities just a few decades ago.

Abortion

One of the most devastating outgrowths of the "Peter Pan" boy/men culture is that these boy/men (not fathers) are impregnating women. Fathers protect, promote and provide for their offspring; they are valiant defenders of their families. True fathers would rather burn down the hospital than let some "doctor" tear his baby, piece by piece, from the womb of his woman! In fact, you don't want to find yourself between a father and his family; it's one way to get yourself hurt. Even the kindest of fathers has a superhero switch that flips on automatically when he senses danger to his daughters or sons.

I remember one of these times in my life. My sixteen-year-old daughter wanted to date a new "Christian" who had moved down the street from us. I was adamantly against the idea, but my daughter persisted as only a daddy's girl can. Finally, I agreed to meet this young guy, talk to him and then make my decision.

A few nights later, my daughter nervously introduced him to me. "Dad," she said with her voice cracking, "this is Henry. He's the one I was telling you about."

74

Henry reached out to shake my hand. I grasped his hand tightly and looked into his eyes. "Nice to meet you, Henry," I replied. Still squeezing his hand, I said, "Henry, this is my daughter, and I am very protective of my kids. If you so much as touch my daughter, I will break both your arms! Do we understand each other, son?"

Henry laughed nervously and nodded his head yes, while I maintained a tight grip on his hand. "Henry," I repeated, deepening my voice, "I'm not kidding. If you even hold my daughter's hand, I will find out, I will come after you and I will break both your arms! Clear?"

"Yes, sir, *very clear*," he answered, his smile fleeing his face.

"Good," I said, squeezing his hand tighter before letting him go. "Let me know where you're going, and have her home by 11:00 p.m."

"Yes, sir . . . okay, man . . . I'll have her home on time," he blurted out.

My daughter stared at the ground through the entire conversation, embarrassed by my display of protection for her. She wasn't very happy with me. They dated one time and he never asked her out again, which was just fine with me. Sometime later, he got some other girl pregnant. His arms weren't broken, so I assume his girlfriend had no daddy.

I'm not suggesting that threatening the young man was the right approach, although it was effective in Henry's case. I'm trying to point out in a rather humorous way that dads protect their daughters . . . it's just the way it is.

Abortion is stealing a life from the womb of a woman. But abortion isn't primarily a sin of motherhood, as is commonly thought. It is the result of a severely broken society, a fatherless community rooted in boys who never made the journey to manhood. It is a manifestation of the Peter Pan man who can't find the courage to step up to the plate of responsibility when the game of life is on the line, because his manhood hasn't germinated in the soil of masculinity.

> **Abortion isn't primarily a sin of motherhood. . . . It is the result of a severely broken society, a fatherless community rooted in boys who never made the journey to manhood.**

In modern history, there has never been more urgency to create rites of passage for boys to become men than there is right now. It is incumbent upon this generation of fathers to shift this destructive boy/men dynamic we are seeing and to rebuild, reform and revive a healthy culture of manhood. This is our charge—the mandate of the men in this twenty-first century.

Recognizing the Rite of Passage

What does the rite of passage mean in the twenty-first century? Is the rite of passage just a ritual that magically turns a boy into a man? The answer is no. The rite of passage *must* be acknowledged and recognized by adults in authority. Let me tell a short story that will help explain what needs to take place in order for young men and women to feel like adults. Many years ago, a leader and his wife reached out to me for some help. Their daughter, who was in her thirties and was married with four children, suddenly wanted nothing to do with her parents.

I knew their daughter to be a great lady, and I was surprised by her attitude. A few weeks later, I met with the three of them in my office. I began the session with all three by having their daughter share what was going on in her heart. She said, "Mom, whenever I'm around you, you talk down to me. You tell me how to raise my kids and how I should treat my husband."

Before she could finish her statement, her mother interrupted her. She put her hand on her daughter's knee, looked into her eyes and said in a loving voice, "Well, honey, you will always be my little girl."

Bingo! I figured out what was wrong. I turned to her mother and said, "Look at your daughter. Does she look like a little girl?"

"No!" she responded, taken aback.

"It's because she's not!" I said. "She's a woman, a wife and a mother. But you need her to remain a little girl because you don't know how to be a mother to a woman; you only know how to be a mother to a little girl. You want to keep her small so you feel needed. Your daughter has been trying to tell you that she is *all grown up* for years, but you refuse to acknowledge her as a woman. You have given her no rite of passage."

The truth is that this mother had turned her daughter's rite of passage into a trail full of tears, and she didn't even know it. She meant well, but she didn't understand that she had handcuffed her daughter to her Barbie dolls and had undermined womanhood and motherhood in her life. This mom apologized, and her daughter forgave her. The rest is history, and they lived happily ever after.

Stepping-Stones to Manhood

This same dynamic of being handcuffed to childhood is at work in boys who have become men but who aren't acknowledged or treated as men by the important people around them. Practically speaking, what does it take for boys to be welcomed into manhood by men? I have identified what I believe are seven stepping-stones that lead to the rite of passage: (1) to be acknowledged as men, (2) to be treated as men, (3) to be trained as men, (4) to be talked to as men, (5) to be recognized as having what it takes to handle a man's responsibility (to be believed in as adults), (6) to be invited to the "man table" with other men, and (7) to have ownership of their lives transferred from other adults to themselves. Let's look at each of these a little more closely.

1. To be acknowledged as men

My grandmother and grandfather owned a farm in Oakdale, California, where I lived and worked during the summers of my teenage years. In my second summer living on the farm, when I was sixteen, my grandfather told me, "I want you to drive the tractor this year during the harvest. Use the tractor to pick up the full bins and load them on the flatbed truck."

Operating the tractor was reserved for men, so I understood that this was my grandfather's way of acknowledging my manhood.

2. To be treated as men

Our kids were required to be in bed by 10:00 p.m. on school nights in our home. When they turned sixteen, we dropped the curfew and they could stay up as late as they wanted. Here was the kicker: They were then responsible for getting themselves up on time for school and catching the bus at the bottom of the road.

One night, I woke up at 3:00 a.m. and could hear the boys still playing video games upstairs. I was excited because I knew they were about to learn a man-sized lesson. When Kathy and I got up that morning, I shared the situation with her, and we agreed to let it be their problem. Sure enough, I heard the bus come and go without the front door of our house opening and closing, and I knew the end was near. Ten minutes later, one of the boys came into our room and asked for a ride.

"Sorry, buddy, there are no rides available today," I answered nonchalantly.

He looked over at his mom, hoping to find some mercy, but she nodded in agreement.

"Well, how are we supposed to get to school?" he responded, sounding really frustrated.

"I don't know, son. It's not our problem. You guys have the authority now to stay up as late as you want, but you also have the responsibility to get yourselves to school on time," I said calmly.

By now he was boiling. "*How* do you expect me to get there?"

"I'm not sure, buddy, but I know you and your brother have great minds, and together you'll figure it out," I encouraged.

A little while later, I passed them in my car as they were walking the two miles to school. I beeped my horn as I passed by, but they didn't look up. And they never were late for school again.

Sometimes the rite of passage can feel painful, especially when the world around young guys is treating them as men, but the man in them hasn't fully emerged from boyhood. There is a tendency in us as fathers and mothers to want to save them from themselves and rescue them from the pain of struggling out of the cocoon. But it is necessary for them to push through the cocoon by themselves so that one day they can stretch their wings and fly.

3. To be trained as men

It so important that young men get a behind-the-scenes look at what's happening in our marriages, our finances and the challenges we face in life. So many kids leave their homes believing that their mom and dad never struggled in their relationship, disagreed about finances and/or faced things in life that utterly terrified them. These boys' fantasy folks have left them uninformed and unprepared for the real-life trials that we all face in this earth suit.

4. To be talked to as men

When Jason was in high school, he was flunking a class that was vital for him to pass in order to graduate. He came and talked to me about how unfair his teacher was, and how he had asked her if he could come in after class and get some extra tutoring help from her. But according to Jay, she flat-out refused, and she let him know that she was failing him. He was distraught, and it really pushed all my "protect my kid from the wicked teacher" buttons. I told him I would "take care of her myself tomorrow."

But that night, I went to bed and heard the Lord say, *There are going to be a lot of people in his life who are unfair, and you won't be there to save him. This is not your fight. He is a young man now; let him handle it.*

The next morning, I called him into my room and repeated what the Lord had said to me. (I didn't tell him that the Lord had shared it with me.) He looked disappointed, but I could tell that he felt believed in.

Weeks passed, and I forgot all about it. Then one day I asked him about the situation: "Yo, dude, whatever happened with your teacher?"

"Oh, Dad, she's dying of a terrible disease, so she's been pretty sick. She let me pray for her the day I went in to talk to her. She also explained the subject to me, so I get it now," he replied.

I was stunned! I thought about how close I had been to missing the opportunity to let my son grow up and take responsibility for his life.

5. To be recognized as having what it takes to handle a man's responsibility (to be believed in as adults)

This is the season when our young men need to be affirmed not just as sons, but as men. Mentors, parents and spiritual leaders should be on the hunt in observing young lives to point out and call out the traits that are resident in them for manhood.

6. To be invited to the "man table" with other men

When I was growing up, we would go to my grandfather and grand-mother's house for Thanksgiving and Christmas dinners. The adults sat at the large dinner table that seated about twelve people. The teenagers sat at a couple of card tables that were set up at the end of the big table, and the kids sat in another room, at a table made of plywood that was resting on two sawhorses. At seventeen, I moved out of my parents' house and got my own apartment. I can still remember my grandfather looking over at me at Thanksgiving dinner that year and saying, "Hey, knucklehead, sit up here with the adults." It was our family's rite of passage ritual.

7. To have ownership of their lives transferred from other adults to themselves

This principle of having ownership transferred to them is played out every day in the lives of those who are crossing over into manhood. It's the point in their lives when we stop saving them, waiting on them and picking up after them. It's the time in their history when they must pay their own car insurance, set up their own dentist appointments and buy their own clothes.

An Invitation into Adulthood

These seven stepping-stones that we just looked at will play out differently in different family systems. They will also apply in different ways to young men and young ladies. But each of these steps is vitally important to any young person's rite of passage. They extend an invitation into adulthood and encourage young people to step up to the plate.

The rite of passage is not a onetime ritual, either. It's a culture that invites boys into manhood (and girls into womanhood) and prepares them for the responsibility of adulthood.

This proactive, holistic approach to the rite of passage—especially for boys becoming men—will catapult society into a new era of healthy, peaceful living.

EPIC
TAKEAWAYS

- The rite of passage: God tasks fathers with the duty of preparing boys for manhood. The rite of passage is the process in which men acknowledge that a boy has become a man.

- Players, not leaders: When the journey to manhood is undermined by dysfunctional fathers or derailed by broken families, boy/men become focused on pleasure instead of purpose.

- Can't find a lover: Boy/men see women only as sisters or mothers and are looking for a lady to take care of them, not be a lover.

- Friends with benefits: Boy/men tend to gravitate toward a cohabiting arrangement because it feels more like being friends with benefits rather than being a husband with the responsibility of a family.

- The missing macho Marlboro Man: The Peter Pan Syndrome appeals to many young men who just want to stay little boys and have fun. It is far easier and more comfortable to deny the passage into manhood than to face it (writes author Chris Bruno).

- Stealing a life: Commonly seen as a sin of motherhood, abortion is largely the result of a severely broken society, a fatherless community rooted in boys who never made the journey to manhood.

- Stepping-stones to manhood: Certain steps (detailed in this chapter) are vital to any young person's rite of passage. These steps extend an invitation into adulthood and encourage young people to step up to the plate.

- A new era: A proactive, holistic approach to the rite of passage—especially for boys becoming men—will catapult society into a new era of healthy, peaceful living.

SIX

The Plight of Fatherless Daughters

WHEN WE THINK of men inviting boys into manhood and consider all the negative effects that fatherless boys and guys with no daddies suffer, it's easy to forget the fact that fathers play a very important but often different role in the lives of their daughters. The origin of this epic fatherly calling really begins in the first book of the Bible, which lays the foundation for all of our family and relational values. The book of beginnings, or Genesis, records the creation of humankind like this: "God created man in His own image, in the image of God He created him; male and female He created them" (Genesis 1:27). One of the things we learn from this verse is that it took a male and a female to represent the nature of God. Therefore, if we eliminate one gender from any home, the parenting influence is reduced to just the male or female side of God.

In the case of the fatherless, of course, we have purged the masculine nature of God Himself from the family culture, as a mother can't possibly represent the masculine nature of God the Father. Consequently, not only does fatherlessness affect a daughter's ability to connect with and relate to men, but it also reduces her understanding of her heavenly Father.

> Not only does fatherlessness affect a daughter's ability to connect with and relate to men, but it also reduces her understanding of her heavenly Father.

I know this might sound odd, but a fatherless society feminizes people's understanding of the nature of God. Think about it for a minute. Living without a father can skew your perspective of God. Personally, I think this is the main reason for the overemphasis on God's mercy and the extreme rise of doctrines like universalism in our generation. To be clear, I'm not saying women are promoting these false doctrines. I'm saying a fatherless, feminized society is not holistically representing God, because we are viewing Him through an incomplete lens. The truth is, we don't see God the way He is. Instead, *we tend to view Him the way we are.*

For example, notice that 1 Corinthians 2:16 doesn't say, "I have the mind of Christ." It says, "*We* have the mind of Christ" (emphasis added). It's our collective perspectives that accurately represent Jesus. What's important to keep in mind here is that in their maturation process, fatherless daughters and/or motherless sons often are not exposed to a gender-inclusive, collective perspective of God. How much impact this has on specific children and ultimately on society is hard to know because there are so many other variables. But when 50 percent of a family's foundation is missing, you can bet the house is leaning like the Tower of Pisa!

Daughters in Crisis

This all adds up to a crisis among girls/daughters because, as we mentioned before, men and women are not the same. Consequently, girls who are raised by only a mother (even a great, unoffended mother) often struggle to learn how to relate to men because mothers don't think like fathers!

One of the most important roles of a father in a healthy home is to teach his daughter(s) how to relate to men and how to understand the masculine side of our heavenly Father. Subsequently, in a healthy home, daughters learn how to navigate holistically the competitive, aggressive and protective nature of men. Furthermore, daughters recognize how to help bring balance to a man's masculine nature by observing their mother's interaction with their father. Mothers demonstrate how to temper a man's passion for power and control by bringing their nurturing nature to bear on their husbands.

Another powerful lesson that daughters learn in a healthy home is that even the strongest, most masculine fathers can be inspired and motivated by a woman's tenderness and compassion.

Moreover, daughters take refuge under the protective arms of their father, whereby they come to understand their dad's role in creating safe places and protecting the family. Another powerful lesson that daughters learn in a healthy home is that even the strongest, most masculine fathers can be inspired and motivated by a woman's tenderness and compassion.

Yet in the absence of healthy fathering, these beautiful attributes in a woman can become skewed or twisted, and can be exchanged for manipulation and/or seductive characteristics that are selfish and self-serving. The truth is that most often, our greatest weaknesses are our strengths overemphasized.

Back to the Old Gym

In the opening chapter of this book, I shared with you our turbulent Lewiston youth group journey and how I became a surrogate father to a bunch of kids who had no daddies. I was doing my best to teach these kids life skills, but I also was getting schooled in fatherlessness on a whole new level. I learned right away that fatherless boys can be violent (we'll talk more about this later). The other thing that our Lewiston experience taught us surprised me, however. It's that, sometimes, fatherless girls can become manipulative and seductive. I soon figured out that because men are physically stronger, fatherless women often fear them, not understanding the healthy nature of masculinity. This can lead women to use their sexuality to control the men around them.

Watching this dynamic play out among the youth in the gym every week helped me understand another important aspect of fathering young girls. Fathers are tasked with teaching daughters about the detrimental effects of seduction and manipulation. The culture among even the youngest of those girls in the gym was so openly manipulative and seductive that it scared me. But an even worse part of their culture was the fact that it sometimes celebrated these dark virtues as noble characteristics. Consequently, I began proactively teaching these girls that although seducing a man could make them feel powerful, it would also unlock the lower nature in men and drive them to be self-serving, uncaring and unloving.

My fatherly talks with the girls were direct and a little crude. (Remember, my audience was tough street kids.) I recorded one of these talks in *Moral Revolution: The Naked Truth about Sexual Purity*, the book Jason and I wrote to help people understand purity and restore it in their lives. I want to share that whole talk with you here because it has so many applications to the fatherless generation that we are now battling for as spiritual (and biological) fathers. I told the girls this:

> *Where* you fish for romance and the bait you use to catch a man says a lot about the virtues you live by. If you are fishing the shark-infested waters of bars and parties, especially if you fish with bait that only sharks bite, please don't be shocked when you catch a hammerhead. The type of bait you use often determines the kind of fish you catch. Ladies, if you are trolling for men with your boobs, butt or belly button, you are fishing for them by stimulating their sex drive. A man's sex drive is inspired predominantly through sight, unlike most women's, which is stimulated primarily through touch. [That's why there are stores like Victoria's Secret, but there are no Johnny's Secret stores.] If you use this kind of bait, you will probably catch a man who is not living from the virtues and values that you respect, but instead is thinking with his penis!
>
> Ladies, contrary to the popular stereotype in our culture, there are men who are pure. They have trained their bodies and minds to obey the restraints required by the virtues that they have embraced. And they are going to be attracted to the same kind of woman. When you dress provocatively, a vir-

tuous man believes that you are primarily interested in attracting sex, not a respectful relationship. The guys that desire a lady who has values, virtues and assets beyond the bedroom will not be attracted to someone trolling for sharks. In fact, you are torturing the virtuous men around you when you dress like a Victoria's Secret mannequin. So ask yourself the question, "Why am I dressing like this?" Is your inner person so empty, bare and bankrupt that you have nothing to offer a virtuous man?

It may feel great to receive admiration and attention from men when you put your body on display. But you need to know or remember that this admiration is totally superficial. It is the same kind of admiration that they have for any other beautiful *object*. If you want to be admired and respected for who you are as a person, then you need to present your physical body in a way that sends that message. When the Federal Reserve picks up the cash from banks, they don't stack it in a sports car, put the top down and drive through town showing it off. No, instead they carry it in an armored vehicle because it is so valuable. They could rush it to the vault faster in a Ferrari, but there is a much better chance of getting the bucks to the bank in a Brinks truck.

Ladies, the moral of this story is, *if it isn't for sale, don't advertise!* I don't mean that you should embrace the spirit of ugly or that you shouldn't look beautiful, dress nicely or smell like a million bucks. I am simply saying that there is a huge difference between looking pretty and being sexy. Even the Bible acknowledges women who were extraordinarily attractive. It says that Queen Esther and Jacob's wife Rachel were beautiful in "form and face" (Esther 2:7; Genesis 29:17). They had nice bodies. Not only that, the Bible also recognizes many other women who God Himself calls *beautiful*. Please do not hear me telling you to get religious or to become some kind of prude. I am telling you to be conscientious about how you are presenting your body to people. Whether you mean to or not, you need to know that when you wear tight clothes, short dresses, low-cut shirts or blouses that expose your belly, it isn't sending a message that you want people to be attracted to you as a person. Rather, it tells them that you want them to see you as a sexual object.

Of course, let's be realistic here, there will always be a few fools who try to rob Brinks trucks even though they are armored, and likewise, we all know that there will always be virtue-less, horny suckers who will manage to sexualize anything that walks, no matter how she dresses. You can't really do much about that. The more you grow as a person, the less that superficial attention will hold any interest for you. You will naturally communicate to those around you that you respect them as people and that you expect them to do the same for you.

Anyone who wants a lifelong relationship should have the common sense to look around and realize that everyone on the planet is aging. Physical attraction and sex alone simply cannot be the foundation for a relationship that has any hope of longevity. It is wisdom to invest in becoming a person whose inner qualities will continue to grow stronger and more beautiful as you age. Think about it, girls, do you really want to live with someone the rest of your life who married you for your body? Have you ever thought about the pressure of what it would be like to age with a "girl watcher"? What is your man going to do when a more beautiful woman comes along? Remember the way you attracted him in the first place? Pretty scary!

Ladies, real men are attracted to women who take an honest interest in them and see the treasure that lies in the depths of their hearts. The truth is that most men are pretty insecure in the presence of a true princess. They need some reassurance that you see something valuable in them and believe in them. What I have observed over the years is that the most physically attractive women are not usually the ones who get married first. More often, they [the first ones married] are the ones who know how to make men feel special, valued and gifted—the ones who capture their hearts. It's really not that hard to make a man feel this way. Just taking a sincere interest in someone and asking the right questions to discover his true passion goes a long way toward breaking down the walls of fear and insecurity.

Sometimes, it seems like women who are pure protect themselves with walls of indifference and then wonder why men don't take an interest in them. It isn't necessary to be a cold fish or to conduct yourself in a businesslike manner to protect your purity. You can be inviting and friendly without being sexy.[1]

Most of the girls I was talking to were fatherless, and most of them had never heard anything like what I was telling them about how they "fished" for men. Most of them had not made the connection between the way they dressed and acted and the kind of men they were reeling in—not keepers, but hammerhead sharks! These girls had no idea how to present themselves as both beautiful and worthy of respect.

The same is true of most of the young girls of today. They need straight talk from a father figure who can help them navigate the shark-infested waters of our current culture.

The Me Too Movement

It's important to stress here that women are *not* responsible for the morality (or immorality) of men. Women should respect themselves, as we talked about already, but men are responsible to manage their sex drive no matter how sensual or sexual the culture is around them. It's never right to blame a woman for a man's inappropriate behavior. I hear people say, "Well, she had it coming," as if a woman is responsible for being raped or sexually assaulted. That's ridiculous! In fact, Jesus had a strong exhortation for men:

> You have heard that it was said, "You shall not commit adultery"; but I say to you that everyone who looks at a woman with lust for her has already committed adultery with her in his heart. If your right eye makes you stumble, tear it out and throw it from you; for it is better for you to lose one of the parts of your body, than for your whole body to be thrown into hell. If your right hand makes you stumble, cut it off and throw it from you; for it is better for you to lose one of the parts of your body, than for your whole body to go into hell.
>
> Matthew 5:27–30

Jesus delivered the strongest exhortation on morality ever spoken by anyone in the history of the world. He said there is *no excuse* for men to be sexualizing women. He said it's better to have no eyes or hands than to allow lust to take you down.

The American Me Too movement that emerged in 2017 is rightly rooted in exposing the sexual abuse men have propagated on women for decades, or even for centuries. So many women have been forced into sex by their bosses, managers, boyfriends and/or leaders. In fact, the sexual abuse of women in the workplace has become a pandemic—literally the norm in places like Hollywood.

Nobody personifies this immoral culture better than the comedian Bill Cosby. I grew up listening to Cosby and had every one of his records. Our family watched *The Cosby Show* religiously. I was *shocked* by the sexual allegations that were levied against this man. He was a fatherly role model for an entire generation of men. As more and more women came forward with allegations of being drugged and raped, and as the things they were saying proved to be true, something died in me. Of course, my hero was defrocked, and his evil was exposed, but there was something deeper that took place in me, something hard to explain. It was as if my hope for humanity was on trial in the courtroom of my soul. A man who seemed like a beacon of light in a society that was moving like a freight train toward the abyss of immorality was himself infected by the same evil.

Jesus put it best: "If then the light that is in you is darkness, how great is the darkness!" (Matthew 6:23).

Holy Affection

In spite of my fallen hero, the Lord actually challenged me to be a beacon of light in the midst of the deep darkness of a culture that has lost its way. He specifically urged me to be a godly, purehearted, noble man who could be trusted with the daughters of God. This was tested one day when I entered our church sanctuary and noticed six young ladies standing at the back of the room, just hanging out, laughing and talking. As I drew closer, I recognized them as some of my ministry school students. I thought to myself, *Wow, those girls are so beautiful.* I decided to make my way over to them and tell them how pretty they were. But as I started to walk toward them, a quiet voice suddenly spoke in my head: *You'd better be careful. What will people think? People will think you are sexualizing those girls! They will not trust your motives. Caution! Caution! Be careful! Warning! Warning!*

I started to turn around and go the other way, when I heard another voice in my head saying, *You are not sexualizing those girls. Your motives are pure. You have never had sex with anyone except your wife (even in your mind) for more than 46 years. You are a father to them. Your affection for them is holy.*

A war raged inside me. I stood there paralyzed, not sure what I should do. All of a sudden, I had a vision of my two daughters, Jaime and Shannon. Jaime and Shannon are both beautiful young women and have always been best friends. Jaime is eighteen months older than Shannon, and they grew up living in the same room together (along with their huge German shepherd, Samson, who used to get into their beds and push them onto the

90

floor). But they had very different experiences when it came to dating and interacting with boys. Although they were both very attractive, Shannon got all the dates, and no one *ever* asked Jaime out. If there was some kind of social event going on in our town, five or six guys would invite Shannon to go with them, but no one would ask Jaime.

The phone would ring off the hook for Shannon, and after a while, Jaime refused to answer the phone because the pain of rejection was so great. When the young men would come to the house to pick up Shannon, Jaime would run upstairs, throw herself on her bed and bawl her eyes out. I would run upstairs behind her and hold her in my arms. She would bury her head in my chest and say through her tears, "Daddy, what's wrong with me? Is there something wrong with me? Daddy, am I ugly? Daddy, am I pretty?"

I would say, "Jaime, you are soooo beautiful! You are such an amazing young woman. But God is hiding you until the right man comes along. You'll see. Your prince will come along someday soon. Now, get dressed up. I'm taking you on a date!"

She would get dressed up, and I would take her out and show her a great time. I took her on more dates than I took Kathy on in those years. A few years later, Jaime met her prince, named Marty, just as I said she would. He is a gentle, loving man—a man worth the wait. He loves God and Jaime, and he is dedicated to his family. I am very proud of them. They are senior pastors of a thriving church on the coast of California, and they have three wonderful children: Mesha, Micah and Alona.

As I came out of this vision of my daughters, I had a revelation. The world is full of Jaime types— beautiful women and handsome men who seem to be hidden for

> I stood there wondering how many of the half-dozen girls in front of me had no daddy at home who could remind them of their beauty during their hidden years.

one reason or another. This revelation brought tears to my eyes, and I stood there wondering how many of the half-dozen girls in front of me had no daddy at home who could remind them of their beauty during

> At that moment, I decided that as long as my heart was pure, I would never let the world dictate my behavior again.

their hidden years. I wondered what would have happened to Jaime if I had not been there to comfort her in those days. Would she have looked for love in all the wrong places, subjecting herself to the sexual desires of men to try to mend her broken heart? I hoped not!

Finally, I couldn't take it anymore. At that moment, I decided that as long as my heart was pure, I would never let the world dictate my behavior again. I turned around and went back to the place where those girls were standing. "You girls are so beautiful!" I said. "I mean it. You ladies are awesome. I'm so very proud of all of you!"

They giggled as though I had embarrassed them a little, but their countenances told the real story. They were beaming as they thanked me for the compliment. Those girls were different from that day on.

Perversion's Ecosystem

What I realized through this experience is that perversion has an ecosystem that sustains, perpetuates and nurtures itself. As perversion grows in a society, people begin to withhold their affection so they won't be perceived as sexual predators. As people withhold their affection, a famine of love begins to grow in the land. In a society starving for affection, love-deprived people begin to lower their sexual standards to obtain some affection. As they break down their moral barriers to do this, perversion increases. This, of course, causes even more people to withhold their love, and the beat goes on and on. Thousands of years ago, the wisest king ever born, King Solomon, wrote, "To a famished man any bitter thing is sweet" (Proverbs 27:7). To love-famished people, even perverted affection is better than no love at all.

One of the manifestations of this perverted ecosystem in which we live is that the line between sex and love has become so blurred that people speak of them as if they are the same thing. There is a huge difference between making love and "screwing" someone. *Sex is not directly related to love on any level.* As a matter of fact, saying that sex is love is like saying that because you flew in a plane, you're an astronaut.

> **Sex is not directly related to love on any level. As a matter of fact, saying that sex is love is like saying that because you flew in a plane, you're an astronaut.**

There are several ramifications and manifestations of misunderstanding the difference between sex and love. The most obvious is that people who have been taught that sex is love will think that someone is showing them love when that person is having sex with them. If this were even remotely true, prostitutes would be the most loved people on the planet. I shouldn't have to tell you that this isn't true. Tina Turner sang a song famously titled "What's Love Got to Do with It?" The answer to that is that love has everything to do with it!

The exciting truth is that as fathers return home and families become whole and healthy, fatherly affection will become the standard—the renewed normal in society. This is my prayer, mission and mandate.

EPIC
TAKEAWAYS

- A skewed perspective: Since mothers can't possibly represent the masculine nature of God the Father, fatherlessness feminizes people's understanding of the nature of God.
- Dads, step into your role: One of the most important roles of a father in a healthy home is to teach his daughter(s) how to relate to men and how to understand the masculine side of our heavenly Father.
- Seduction and manipulation: Seducing a man can make fatherless girls feel powerful. But underneath, they don't know how to relate to men—especially noble men who will treat them as valuable on more than a superficial level.
- Pick the right fishing hole, girls: If you are fishing the shark-infested waters of bars and parties, especially if you fish with seductive bait that only sharks bite, don't be shocked when you catch a hammerhead. The type of bait you use often determines the kind of fish you catch.
- Beautiful in "form and face": Even the Bible acknowledges women who were extraordinarily attractive, but the most physically attractive women are not usually the ones who get married first. It is usually the women who know how to make men feel special, valued and gifted who capture their hearts.
- She didn't "have it coming" to her: Men are responsible to manage their sex drive, no matter how sensual or sexual the culture is around them. It's never right to blame a woman for a man's inappropriate behavior.
- Holy affection: If a man's motives are pure, he can act as a father to young women and encourage them, without sexualizing them.
- The ecosystem of perversion: As perversion increases, people withhold their affection so that they won't be perceived as sexual predators. A famine of love grows in the land, and love-deprived

folks then begin to lower their sexual standards to obtain affection. As they break down their moral barriers, perversion increases . . . and the beat goes on and on.

- A renewed normal in society: As fathers return home and families become whole and healthy, fatherly affection will become the standard once again.

SEVEN

Prepare for Reentry

IT'S EASY TO GET EXCITED about fathers returning home and reconciling with their sons and daughters, but if the reentry is going to go well, there will need to be preparation on so many levels. Building trust and healing wounds are just a couple of the challenges we will face in the next fifty years. Men must learn how to be fathers and husbands, while girls become daughters and boys become sons. The million-dollar question is, How does a generation raised in a proverbial orphanage migrate home and successfully create healthy families for the first time in three decades?

This was the question that was pressing on my soul one Sunday morning as I was preparing to lead prayer at Bethel Church. I suddenly heard this phase in my spirit: *Prepare for reentry!*

I stood there trying to understand the divine context of this apparent prophetic proclamation, *Prepare for reentry!* Abruptly, the prodigal son's story began to play in my head like a short film or a divine documentary. The tale is familiar to most of us: A farmer has two sons, of which the younger (the prodigal) is wayward, rebellious and worldly. He decides to exit his dad's house with his (supposed) inheritance. He parties it up with prostitutes and pimps, and soon he's stone-broke. Half starving to death, the kid winds up working at the pig farm, slopping hogs.

It's quite ironic that, in this prodigal's pilgrimage, he got stuck at a pig farm, as the Jews in those days weren't supposed to eat pork, which was unclean. So that place became a prophetic monument to the boy's misery . . . a son in rebellion, living an unclean life, feeding unclean animals, and all because he entertained unclean thoughts in his very clean father's house!

In the midst of his misery, this young man has an epiphany: *What the heck am doing at this pig palace when I could be living at my father's farm?* So he comes to himself and heads home.

This is where the story gets really good! The dad has prepared for his son's reentry because he has been living in hopeful observation. Furthermore, the father, understanding that shame could derail his boy's reunion, and *seeing* his son a long way off, runs out to greet him. Throwing his strong arms around his son, he begins kissing him.

The boy, riddled with disgrace and wallowing in humiliation, spills his guts: "Father, I have sinned against heaven and in your sight; I am no longer worthy to be called your son" (Luke 15:21).

But his father has envisioned this reunion and has rehearsed his son's reentry a million times in his imagination. In utter exhilaration, this dad shouts to his servants, "Quickly bring out the best robe and put it on him, and put a ring on his hand and sandals on his feet; and bring the fattened calf, kill it, and let us eat and celebrate; for this son of mine was dead and has come to life again; he was lost and has been found" (verses 22–24).

What is obscure but powerful here is this father's influence over the community's mindset concerning his son's reentry. First of all, he dictates the narrative of his son's return: "It's time to celebrate!" You might be thinking, *What?! This rebellious punk wasted his father's wealth on loose living and dragged the family name through the pig trough! Furthermore, he trashed his relationship with God in favor of wild women and drunken parties—and now the kid runs out of cash, so he wants to drag his sorry butt home? No way!*

But the prodigal's father wasn't tolerating that kind of thinking. Instead, he requires the community to participate in his son's restoration: "*You* put the robe on his back, the sandals on his feet and the ring on his finger!" The father doesn't only restore him; he orchestrates the young man's restoration so that the entire community reestablishes the son's nobility (the robe), his purity (the sandals) and his authority (the ring).

Then the father shouts, "Hey, guys, kill the fattened calf I've been raising for this special occasion, and let's get this party started!" This is such an important step because the son is not left to try to work out his relationship with the family's employees, his peer group or the community. The father has established the attitude of reemergence for his son so that there will be no punishment, no cold shoulders, no confrontation or rebuke . . . just a big party with music, eating, drinking and dancing.

The servants and the community apparently embrace the father's mindset, but the father has an older son who isn't happy about his dad's attitude toward his brother's reentry. The older brother, separated from the family and drowning his poverty mentality in hard work and self-righteousness, hears the people partying from his field of frustration and orders his servant to tell him what's going on.

"Your brother has come," the servant replies, "and your father has killed the fattened calf because he has *received* him back safe and sound" (verse 27, emphasis added).

Livid, the pretentious elder brother refuses to join the celebration. But the wise father, true to his nature and unafraid of confrontation, journeys out again . . . this time to meet his older son in the field and implore him to join the festivities.

But the older son answers, "Look! For so many years I have been serving you and I have never neglected a command of yours; and yet you have never given me a young goat, so that I might celebrate with my friends; but when *this son of yours* came, who has devoured your wealth with prostitutes, you killed the fattened calf for him" (verses 29–30, emphasis added).

The elder brother's reply is telling. Did you notice his description of the prodigal as *this son of yours*, not *this brother of mine*? His bitterness has detached and disconnected him from thinking like a member of a family. But the wise father reassures his older son of his own place in his heart, saying, "Son, you have always been with me, and all that is mine is yours" (verse 31). In other words, "Your brother's restoration doesn't in any way diminish your place with me. I gave your brother the fattened calf, but you own the farm!"

Check out the climax of the father's salutation: "But we had to celebrate and rejoice, for *this brother of yours* was dead and has begun to live, and was lost and has been found" (verse 32, emphasis added). Did you catch it, *this brother of yours*? The dad just took his wayward son and reconnected him to the elder brother. The implication to the elder son was that "You, son, also have responsibility for your *brother's* reentry because he is part of your family." The truth is that it's so easy to be critical of something you don't have to participate in. Yet owning the problem is half the solution.

Lessons from the Prodigal's Pilgrimage

What can we learn from the prodigal's pilgrimage that will help us prepare for this epic reconciliation that needs to take place in the families of our generation? First, we must embrace this father's faith for reconciliation, which he demonstrates through his expectation of his son's return. He was able to meet his son while the young man was still a long way from home because this father was watching in earnest expectation.

I think it's important to point out here that this father had faith for his son's return, his repentance, his change of heart. He wasn't guided by unsanctified mercy, accepting his son's sinful lifestyle to woo the boy homeward. And his son respected his father's nobility and understood that he couldn't bring his immoral lifestyle to the father's farm, knowing prostitutes and pigs would be unwelcome there. Instead, there is an unspoken understanding in the story that he must acknowledge his sin and forsake his lifestyle of perversion in exchange for his family's noble virtues.

Sometimes our love for people is not rooted in faith for their return. Instead, in fear we undermined their process of repentance by circumventing the necessary journey and renegotiating our terms of endearment. Metaphorically speaking (and at the risk of sounding rude), because we reason that it's our holy standard that is keeping the prodigals away, we turn the farm into a whorehouse to entice them to return home. Furthermore, we lack faith in the Holy Spirit's ability to convict them of their sin and give them the grace they need to change. Somehow, in our zeal we mistakenly believe that the goal of God is to get them back in the building, when in fact God's goal is repentance . . . for them to change their way of thinking, and to agree with their father's noble lifestyle.

The apostle Paul said it best: "Do you think lightly of the riches of His kindness and tolerance and patience, not knowing that the kindness of God leads you to repentance?" (Romans 2:4). Let me point out again that God's kindness leads to *repentance*, which leads to restoration. But reentry without repentance is not restoration; it is human sympathy, not God-ordained compassion.

The wayward son's repentance is evidenced in his confession: "Father, I have sinned against heaven and in your sight; I am no longer worthy to be called your son." The confession of sin is paramount to the reentry process because it's the catalyst for

> **Reentry without repentance is not restoration; it is human sympathy, not God-ordained compassion.**

grace, which is the power to change. The apostle John put it like this: "If we say that we have no sin, we are deceiving ourselves and the truth is not in us. If we confess our sins, He is faithful and righteous to forgive us our sins and to cleanse us from all unrighteousness" (1 John 1:8–9). The challenge is that you can't separate *cleansing from unrighteousness* from *confession*. Therefore, if we normalize sin and refuse to admit that what we are doing is wrong, we undermine the power of *grace*, the supernatural ability to change.

Nowhere is this personified more than in the "gay Christian" movement. Contrary to very popular opinion, homosexuality is a temptation that you resist or give in to; it's not a genetic predisposition akin to an ethnic group. The Bible very clearly lists homosexuality as sin that is only overcome by God's mercy and grace. The difficulty is that the only way to receive mercy (which means you don't get what you deserve) is to acknowledge that you deserve to be punished, since mercy is only reserved for the guilty.

It Takes Two

What I am pointing out here is twofold: The prodigals (fathers, sons, daughters or even mothers) must repent, not *just* return home. But conversely, fathers (the community and family) must ditch their religious, judgmental attitudes toward those who fail. If family members are punishers, it's unlikely that prodigal fathers, sons, daughters and mothers are going to want to renew their relationships. In fact, the fear of rejection—i.e., reaching out and the family not reaching back—is often what hinders or halts a prodigal's reentry.

The apostle Paul highlights the main secret of reconciliation in this passage:

> Therefore if anyone is in Christ, he is a new creature; the old things passed away; behold, new things have come. Now all these things are from God, who reconciled us to Himself through Christ and gave us the ministry of reconciliation, namely, that God was in Christ reconciling the world to Himself, *not counting their trespasses against them*, and He has committed to us the word of reconciliation.
>
> Therefore, we are ambassadors for Christ, as though God were making an appeal through us; we beg you on behalf of Christ, be reconciled to God.
>
> 2 Corinthians 5:17–20, emphasis added

Did you catch the secret of reconnection? God's policy of reconciliation is "not counting their trespasses against them." He goes on to call us ambassadors of reconciliation who appeal to the wayward on Christ's behalf. In other words, the preparation for the reconcilers (those living at the father's farm, so to speak) is to embrace the kind of forgiveness that restores the standard of righteousness and opens the door for the reentry.

This truth was highlighted to me many years ago when my kids were teenagers. One day I became angry with Kathy and spoke disrespectfully to her. These kinds of situations are rare in our marriage, but nevertheless it happened. Worse yet, one of my sons was watching. That day, I apologized to Kathy for my complete disrespect and she quickly forgave me. But when I got in bed that night, I heard the Lord say to me, *You asked Kathy to forgive you, but you didn't ask your son to forgive you. If you don't let him know you failed, he will think it's okay to treat women with disrespect.*

So the next morning, I mustered my courage, gathered the kids together in the living room and asked Kathy and each of the kids to forgive me.

Of course, our teenagers weren't excited about sitting in the living room while viewing an object lesson on forgiveness from their dad, but it was important anyway.

"Will you please forgive me for being rude to your mother?" I questioned while staring at each of them individually.

"Yes, we forgive you," they each proclaimed in an exasperated tone. "Can we go now?" they begged.

About a week later, one of our boys came into the kitchen, not knowing I was around the corner in the bedroom. He began talking rudely to Kathy with his arrogant teenage attitude. I immediately walked in on him and said, "Dude, you do not have permission to talk to my wife like that. You got that?"

He quickly snapped back, "You were rude to Mom the other day yourself!"

"Yes," I countered, "but you forgave me. Forgiveness restores the standard. When you forgave me, you gave away your right to act the same way, because your forgiveness restored me back to the place of honor. I repented. Repentance means to be *restored to the pinnacle*, the high place."

Staring at me with a huge question mark on his face, yet determined not to get the rest of my sermon by asking the obvious question rolling around in his brain, he turned to his mom and said, "I'm sorry for being rude!"

I'm pretty sure he didn't entirely understand what happened that morning, but it's paramount that you and I do! The truth is, if you don't understand forgiveness, then the lowest point, the worst mistake or the stupidest thing you've ever done in life becomes your high-water mark. For example, if you were immoral as a teenager and later on in life you have teenagers yourself, you won't have the confidence to correct them for their poor sexual choices, because you failed in that area. You might reason that you would be a hypocrite to correct them for something you did at their age. But the truth

> **The truth is, if you don't understand forgiveness, then the lowest point, the worst mistake or the stupidest thing you've ever done in life becomes your high-water mark.**

is that failures you have repented of are no longer the standard you must bow to. When you asked God and those you hurt to forgive you, forgiveness catapulted you back to the high place in God and restored you to the standard of holiness in and through you. Otherwise, the worst day of your life would become your leadership ceiling, the highest place that you have the right to lead others to. So remember this: You are better than your worst day!

Prophetic Acts

When I was leading the prayer time on the Sunday morning I mentioned at this chapter's start, I felt the Lord tell me to instruct the people who were longing for the return of a loved one to do a prophetic act. I proclaimed, "Some of you need to prepare the bedroom for your son's or daughter's return. Others of you need to go out and buy the ingredients of your wayward husband's favorite meal so that you can prophetically prepare for his reentry."

I know you may be thinking that I lost my marbles or fell off my rocker and hit my dang head. But let me tell you the rest of that Sunday's story. Two hours after I prophetically proclaimed out loud, "Prepare for reentry," one of my grandsons who hadn't been following the Lord for years texted this to me: "Papa, I'm not doing good. I'm making bad choices. I need your help. Can we meet?" His life turned around that week, and he enrolled in the Bethel School of Supernatural Ministry, where he is thriving as I write this chapter!

Okay, you concede, *where are the prophetic acts in the Bible and what are they, anyway?* A prophetic act is an exploit of faith where we call things that are not as though they are (see Romans 4:17). We often articulate it like this: Physical obedience brings spiritual release. For example, it's apparent that the father in the prodigal story was saving a special calf, a robe, a ring and sandals because he was anticipating his son's return. He didn't just believe God for his boy's return; he prepared in faith, anticipating God's redemption in their situation.

Another of my favorite prophetic acts in the Bible takes place in Elisha's encounter with the bankrupt widow. Here is the story:

Now a certain woman of the wives of the sons of the prophets cried out to Elisha, "Your servant my husband is dead, and you know that your servant feared the LORD; and the creditor has come to take my two children to be his slaves." Elisha said to her, "What shall I do for you? Tell me, what do you have in the house?" And she said, "Your maidservant has nothing in the house except a jar of oil." Then he said, "Go, borrow vessels at large for yourself from all your neighbors, even empty vessels; do not get a few. And you shall go in and shut the door behind you and your sons, and pour out into all these vessels, and you shall set aside what is full." So she went from him and shut the door behind her and her sons; they were bringing the vessels to her and she poured. When the vessels were full, she said to her son, "Bring me another vessel." And he said to her, "There is not one vessel more." And the oil stopped. Then she came and told the man of God. And he said, "Go, sell the oil and pay your debt, and you and your sons can live on the rest."

2 Kings 4:1–7

I guess the obvious revelation here is that the prophet required her to gather jars for oil she didn't have. Her physical obedience in gathering the jars inspired a spiritual release in the creative miracle of the multiplied oil.

Let me be clear that I am not talking about performing some hocus-pocus magic trick here. Nor am I just trying to get you to prepare for a prodigal's return (which may be very wise to do). What I am saying is to get alone with God and ask Him if there is an "act of faith" that would open up the spiritual dimensions and inspire heavenly help. This may be

> **A prophetic act is an exploit of faith where we call things that are not as though they are. . . . Physical obedience brings spiritual release.**

hard to swallow, but there are invisible forces at work in our visible world, and some of those forces are opposed to us. In fact, these evil forces (i.e., demons) want to kill your loved ones, destroy your family and steal your legacy. That's why so much of what goes on in the life of disconnected fathers, mothers and children is often irrational—because it's being driven by an unseen yet powerful enemy. (I wrote an entire book on this subject, titled *Spirit Wars: Winning the Invisible Battle against Sin and the Enemy*

[Chosen, 2012]. For the sake of not being redundant, I encourage you to read that book.)

Final Words

Let me close this chapter by challenging you to believe God for your miracle of reconciliation, and by encouraging you not to lose hope, no matter your circumstances. The more hopeless your situation seems, the greater the glory of your restoration will be.

Let me leave you with this amazing story. Many years ago, during worship in Weaverville on a Sunday morning, I heard the Lord tell me that there was a person in the room who had not seen his son in nine years. I stood up, went to the mic and proclaimed, "There is a man here who hasn't seen his son in nine years. God told me to tell you that before the day is over, you are going to hear from him and he is coming home!"

> The more hopeless your situation seems, the greater the glory of your restoration will be.

Suddenly, a man I barely knew stood to his feet and shouted, "That's me! I haven't heard from my son in nine years. I don't even know if he's alive. But I receive that word for my family."

When the man got home that day, the red light on his answering machine was blinking (pretty old school, right?). He pushed the button on the machine and heard, "Dad, this is me . . . your son Jeff. Dad, I'm hitchhiking through Yreka, and I really want to see you. Here's the number of this phone booth. . . . I'm waiting for your call!"

His father called him back and then made the drive to reconnect. His son moved home for a season, while he got his life together. God did a miracle of reconnection for them, and if He did it for them, then He will surely do it for you, too. *Never give up!*

EPIC
TAKEAWAYS

- *Prepare for reentry*: Men must learn how to be fathers and husbands, while girls become daughters and boys become sons.
- The prodigal's pilgrimage: We must embrace this father's faith for reconciliation—he had faith for his son's return, his repentance and his change of heart.
- Unsanctified mercy versus repentance: There needs to be an unspoken understanding that a prodigal must acknowledge sin and forsake a perverted lifestyle in exchange for the family's noble virtues.
- Sympathy versus compassion: God's kindness leads to *repentance*, which leads to restoration. But reentry without repentance isn't restoration; it's human sympathy, not God-ordained compassion.
- Evidence of repentance: Confession of sin is paramount to the reentry process because it's the catalyst for *grace*, which is the supernatural power to change. You can't separate *cleansing from unrighteousness* from *confession* (see 1 John 1:8–9).
- Reentry—it takes two: The prodigals (fathers, sons, daughters or even mothers) must repent, not *just* return home. But conversely, fathers (the community and family) must ditch their religious, judgmental attitudes toward those who fail.
- Your high-water mark: Failures you have repented of are no longer the standard you must bow to. Asking for forgiveness catapults you back to the high place in God and restores you to the standard of holiness in and through you. You are better than your worst day!
- The power of prophetic acts: People who long for the return of a loved one can do a prophetic act—an exploit of faith where we call things that are not as though they are. The prodigal's father fattened a calf, for example, in expectation of his son's return.
- Get alone with God: Ask God if there is a prophetic "act of faith" that would open up the spiritual dimensions and inspire heavenly

help for the prodigal situation you face. Physical obedience brings spiritual release.

- *Never give up*: Believe God for your miracle of reconciliation and don't lose hope, no matter your circumstances. The more hopeless your situation seems, the greater the glory of your restoration will be.

EIGHT

Paris Trips and Underwear

IT'S EXCITING TO DREAM about the Lord restoring families—fathers reunited with their children and God healing the broken hearts of kids who were abandoned by their dads for a "better" life. Yet most of these reunions include the restoration of a marriage as husbands and wives begin the often long journey of rebuilding trust in their relationship with their spouse. The challenge for so many good men and women, as I stated already, is that they grew up without any role models and therefore have no idea how to be husbands or wives, much less fathers or mothers.

I've sat with hundreds of married couples over the last 22 years and grieved deeply as I listened to their stories. I've often found myself sitting there, wondering where even to start the rebuilding process because so many of them have had no training in relational skills and have no idea how to live together in love and harmony. To make matters worse, couples often don't reach out for help until their marriage is all but over. I can't even tell you how many times I've caught myself thinking, *You guys don't need a counselor; you need an exorcist, or even a resurrection!* Couples often seek counsel only after their *fear* of losing their spouse becomes greater than the *pain* of exposing their dysfunctional relationship to someone.

Here is a great example of the most common challenge married couples face as a side effect of one or both being raised in a fatherless home. Years ago in a counseling session, a couple whom I will call Paula and Mark (not their real names) came into my office. She had grown up in a fairly healthy home, but he had been raised without a dad. She walked into my office with her husband in tow, looking for help. While she was poised and attractive, he slouched in looking unkempt, and his facial expression reeked of *"She drug me in here!"* He nervously shook my hand without making eye contact and plopped down on the couch, as if he had suddenly lost complete control of his legs.

> **Couples often seek counsel only after their *fear* of losing their spouse becomes greater than the *pain* of exposing their dysfunctional relationship to someone.**

They had been married for a while, and for the last miserable decade this wife had tried to convince her husband that they needed to get some help for their marriage. He refused to listen, until the day she finally asked for a divorce. A few minutes into our counseling session, it became clear that Mark didn't want to lose his wife, but he was befuddled by her unhappiness. His ignorance made me feel sorry for him; he clearly had no clue how to please his wife.

Paula's unfiltered dialogue screamed, *"I am done with you, dude!"* She opened the conversation with a relentless rant, rattling off a list of his infractions like a machine gun in a dogfight, while he stared at the floor and looked bewildered. She finished by yelling, *"Every morning for years you've left your underwear on the floor, and I beg you to pick them up and put them in the hamper! But you won't even do that!"*

Finally, Mark's anger overcame his fear. Red-faced, he shouted back, *"I took you to Paris on your dream vacation! I never get credit for any of the big things I do for you!"*

"Yes, but you don't respect me at home!" she countered.

The war was on. Finally, after several minutes I stepped in and stopped the fight. He looked like a whipped dog. "Look at me," I asked him.

"Yeah?" he said, waiting for another beating.

"Mark, you can't fix with a Paris trip what you broke with your underwear," I explained.

He stared at me with tears in his eyes and a clueless question mark on his face, so I continued, "An amazing vacation won't compensate for a lifetime of disrespect. Listen, romantic getaways are important, but you can't build a marriage on events. Relationships thrive on consistency, so if you want a healthy marriage, you will have to do what you do when you feel like it, even when you don't!"

The truth is that this couple represents a large percentage of the troubled marriages I have encountered. Thankfully, the two of them learned how to honor and respect one another. It took a lot of patience and a ton of hard work, but over time they rebuilt their marriage. Sadly, many other couples never do. There are many complex situations in life that often require intervention from a wise counselor. Yet the truth is that most of the time, it's the simple things in life, the "no-brainer" stuff, that is at the core of the majority of divorces. Unfortunately, there are just too many people today who never learn how to love.

Feelings: Facts or Fake News?

Let me digress for a minute and speak to a subject that was at work in Paula and Mark's marriage, and which plagues most of society. As we discussed earlier, society has now elevated feelings above facts, and above virtues, values and even science. Feelings are important; after all, nobody wants Earth to be a Vulcan planet. We are humans, not Spock-like aliens with zero EQ (emotional intelligence quotient), living in an ice cave somewhere in the cosmos. Feelings enrich our lives, bring color to our black-and-white world and give us insights that can transcend logic and reason.

But the nature of feelings is that they aren't (necessarily) rooted in rational deductions or factual conclusions. Instead, they are, as the word itself suggests, *feel + ings . . . ings* that we *feel*. You can't see them, take a blood test or get a CAT scan to confirm that you have them. They just are. Furthermore, we often have very strong feelings about things that prove completely false, or we have very mild feelings about things that are profoundly true and extremely important. My point is that feelings are not a reliable source of how we are doing. Therefore, how we feel is not how we are.

So many people let their feelings dictate their attitudes, their actions and even their identities. The fact is that emotions determine the destiny of a lot of well-meaning people. Some people have even convinced themselves that they're being fake or phony if they feel one way but act another.

> We often have very strong feelings about things that prove completely false, or we have very mild feelings about things that are profoundly true and extremely important.

Let's get down and dirty in the garden of reality. Have you ever made up a story in your mind that scared the heck out of you, only to figure out a few hours later that the whole thing was just an illusion? I can't even count the number of times that has happened to me. For instance, recently I sent a text message to one of my team members asking him to join us for dinner in a couple of days. A day passed without a response, so I sent a follow-up text reiterating the first text with a little more detail. Another day passed without a response, which was really unlike my friend, who has always been a texting machine. So I sent a little emoji with a confused-looking face. Still, there was no response.

I started feeling really rejected, and I suddenly remembered a conflict this friend and I had had about six months earlier. The conflict turned into a passionate disagreement in my office, but we did work it out later that day. Even though we had connected several times since then, I began to imagine that he somehow had grown offended and didn't want to have anything to do with me. Soon I was debating with him in my head, imagining both sides of the argument. Of course, I always won the debate in my own supreme court of insecurity.

Several more days passed without any response from this friend, and the story in my mind grew more intense and irrational. Finally I said to

Kathy, "I don't care if he ever calls me! I've had it with him. I'm going to fire his butt!"

Kathy tried to inject some reality into my situation, but I refused to let her influence my perspective. I had already tried this person in the court of accusation, and he had lost the case to the jury of suspicion. Another dejected week passed, and abruptly, seemingly out of the blue, my phone blew up with his text messages: "Sorry for the delayed response! I was camping in the mountains for two weeks with my fam and didn't have any cell reception. Love to connect with you and Kathy. We miss you guys tons!"

I felt so stupid. I sheepishly read the text to Kathy, while she stared at me with those convicting eyes. I wish I could say I will never do that kind of thing again, but I understand that feelings are powerful forces in our souls. Feelings are also brilliant lawyers that often argue ridiculous cases and call for factless injunctions in the supreme court of our hearts and minds.

The most troubling aspect of a feelings-led life is how often feelings lie to us and yet how faithfully we trust them. Can you imagine taking the advice of a doctor, dentist, teacher or advisor who lied to you as often as your feelings do? Yikes! Yet feelings literally determine the destiny of millions of people who live completely dysfunctional lives. Anorexic people "feel" fat, despite the quite visible evidence otherwise, while paranoid people "feel" convinced someone is out to get them. Some people are even letting their feelings dictate their gender, despite the genetic, biological and physiological evidence against such far-fetched conclusions. Furthermore, society has so elevated feelings above facts that it demands that we accept the illusions of others as reality. Men are trapped in women's bodies, or vice versa, these illusionists proclaim. *And what is the twenty-first-century scientific proof?* you ask.

Feelings! That's it . . . all the evidence in this case demands that he is a man. But he feels like a woman, so therefore, he is a she. He can have a sex change, but it will only be cosmetic, because he/she has no womb, no ovaries, no eggs and therefore will never bear a child.

Kris, you're off the rails. Where the heck are you going with all of this? you are thinking.

I'm trying to point out how dramatically feelings have affected our culture and how powerfully they dictate the destiny of so many millions

113

of people. It's literally a miracle that marriages work at all in the cesspool of our virtue-less twenty-first-century society.

"I'm Not Feeling It" versus Nobility

We often judge the quality of our marriage by how often we "feel" love for our spouse. The sixties rock group the Righteous Brothers depicted this generation best when they sang the song "You've Lost That Lovin' Feeling." The truth is, feelings are affected by so many things that there's no way you can build anything lasting or meaningful on them.

Imagine building a house in a flood zone that floods every year. Or erecting a beautiful palace out of ice. Or how about constructing the proverbial sandcastle on the edge of the ocean shore? It sounds crazy, but these are great word pictures that illustrate the reality of building and basing the foundation of our relationships on feelings. There will be floods, the heat will come and the tides will rise . . . it's inevitable. Defying the laws of nature is just dumb.

> **The truth is, feelings are affected by so many things that there's no way you can build anything lasting or meaningful on them.**

It doesn't matter if you build a house, a palace or a castle—it may be stunning now, but homelessness is written into your future.

Okay, then, what do we do with these strong feelings? Great question. Here are three principles that will help us navigate our emotional world:

1. Remember it is normal to have seasons in every relationship when you may feel positive emotions, negative emotions or even a lack of emotion. This includes marriage. Don't measure the condition of your marriage by the inconsistency of your feelings.

2. Don't allow how you feel to determine how you behave. Noble people live from virtues and values, meaning that you train your soul to follow your *will* and not your emotions.

3. Recall a time when you were "feeling it" for your spouse, and remember what you did to please him or her in that season. Behave the way you did then when you are with your spouse now.

Potty Training Your Soul

Kris, are you saying I should just stuff my feelings and get over it?

No! What I am pointing out is that the nature of love is *choice*, and the power of love is in your *will*, not your feelings. The goal of a virtuous life is that feelings *follow* choice—choice that is rooted in doing what's right all the time, every day.

It's amazing how this works. You simply tell your soul how you are going to behave and how you are going to feel. Then, in time, the feelings will follow. I call it "potty training your soul."

Here is a crazy example. We have a huge six-year-old German shepherd that we got when he was six weeks old. His name is Samson, and he lives in our house at night. He's a great dog and super fun to be around. He always wakes up in a good mood, which is great for me because I am not the "early bird gets the worm" kind of guy. I am much more like the "second mouse gets the cheese" person. But Samson's first year with us was tough. In fact, we nearly gave him away. He would just pee and poop anywhere and anytime he *felt* like it. It didn't matter to him where—the bedroom floor, the front-room carpet, the office wall . . . when he was *feeling it*, he just did it. I got so tired of stepping in his crap and slipping in his pee that I wanted to kill him! We did everything we knew how to do to potty train this darn dog, but nothing seemed to work. Finally, Kathy found a training video that showed us how to teach Samson to *hold it* and *do it* in the appropriate place and at the right time. This was all part of the normal process of Sammy growing from a puppy into an adult dog, yet it was grueling.

> You simply tell your soul how you are going to behave and how you are going to feel. Then, in time, the feelings will follow. I call it "potty training your soul."

We aren't dogs, of course, but when it comes to our feelings, it's not uncommon for humans to act with the same lack of restraint as a puppy. As I stated earlier, our emotions are wonderful servants but terrible masters. We must learn to *house-train* them so that we don't destroy our long-term, meaningful relationships with urgent messes. I like the way King Solomon put it: "Like a city whose walls are broken through is a person who lacks self-control" (Proverbs 25:28 NIV).

Building on Fault Lines

Of course, there are also times when our feelings aren't fake news; they are telling us the truth. In these cases, no matter how well we manage our inner world, our soul remains troubled. Yet there are effective ways to deal with our destructive, negative and/or troubling emotions. Solomon also said, "A man's discretion makes him slow to anger, and it is his glory to overlook a transgression" (Proverbs 19:11). The word *discretion* here is the Hebrew word *sekel*, which means to be prudent, and to have insight and intelligence, as well as understanding and wisdom. In other words, we don't let our feelings dictate our responses (in this case, anger), because we understand how our choices affect others and ourselves.

This lesson was driven home to me the other day when I walked into my workshop and noticed my tools scattered all over the floor and the workbenches covered in dirt and sawdust. Before I go on, I must admit that I'm a clean freak. I keep pretty much everything I own immaculately organized and spotlessly clean. So this was all the evidence of a nasty intruder, and since I have ten grandkids, six of whom frequently use my shop, I had a pretty good idea who the violator was. I have laid down the shop rules to all of them on several occasions: "If you use the shop, wipe off the tools and put them away where you found them, and then clean up your mess!" Yet the truth is, they often leave the place a mess. Ugh!

I sent a group text to the most common violators of the shop mandates, demanding to know who had left the place a mess this time. A few minutes later, the culprit confessed their sin and offered a two-word apology: "Sorry, Papa." My blood was cooking since this grandchild of mine was the most grievous of shop sinners in the entire family. I had confronted and instructed this child on numerous occasions, to no avail. Now, let me be clear: I don't yell, scream or lose it when I talk to anyone. I am not a hothead. But I am persistent.

I stared at the text response and said out loud, *Lord, give me patience!*

To my surprise, I immediately heard back from the Lord, *You don't need patience; you need love. Love is patient, and if you loved your grandkids the way I called you to love them, then you would be patient!*

The love chapter immediately popped into my brain:

> Love is patient, love is kind and is not jealous; love does not brag and is not arrogant, does not act unbecomingly; it does not seek its own, is not provoked, does not take into account a wrong suffered, does not rejoice in unrighteousness, but rejoices with the truth; bears all things, believes all things, hopes all things, endures all things.
>
> Love never fails.
>
> 1 Corinthians 13:4–8

It took a few days for the full impact of this revelation to settle in my spirit, as I have spent most of my life praying for and seeking the attributes of love. Somehow, I missed the fact that the apostle Paul was describing the *evidence* that love is present in our lives. If we cultivate love in our hearts, the side effects of the agape love of God are patience, kindness and so on. It's impossible to manifest the fruit of a virtue that is not rooted in our hearts.

Think about it like this: If I light a torch, the manifestation of the flame is heat. Heat isn't the flame; heat is the effect of the flame. In the same way, love is the flame, and patience is one of the effects of the flame—a sign that the torch is lit. Trying to be patient with people without loving them is like expecting there to be heat without actually lighting the torch. Metaphorically speaking, God equips each of us with a torch, and He also created the laws of chemistry and physics that

> **Husbands/fathers are tasked with tending the eternal flame that warms the hearts of all of those given into their care.**

make fire possible. But we must light the torch, because love is *always* an act of our will.

Husbands/fathers are the torch that is always to be burning in the midst of the family's front room. Husbands/fathers are tasked with tending the eternal flame that warms the hearts of all of those given into their care. Here is Paul's exhortation to husbands:

> Be subject to one another in the fear of Christ.
>
> Wives, be subject to your own husbands, as to the Lord. For the husband is the head of the wife, as Christ also is the head of the church, He Himself being the Savior of the body. But as the church is subject to Christ, so also the wives ought to be to their husbands in everything.
>
> Husbands, love your wives, just as Christ also loved the church and gave Himself up for her, so that He might sanctify her, having cleansed her by the washing of water with the word, that He might present to Himself the church in all her glory, having no spot or wrinkle or any such thing; but that she would be holy and blameless.
>
> Ephesians 5:21–27

It's important to note here that although Paul's instruction includes *submission* to both husbands and wives, husbands are the only ones who are specifically exhorted to *love*. Of course, for a family to be truly healthy, the husband, wife and children must all love one another. Yet in the context of family, the emphasis and instruction to love is given only to the husband/father, not to the rest of the household. This speaks to the responsibility of husbands/fathers to steward the family flame so that in the unlikely event that the torch of another family member flames out, it might be reignited by the chief lover, the keeper of the fire . . . the father of the family.

EPIC
TAKEAWAYS

- Restoring marriages is vital: So many good men and women have grown up without any role models and therefore have no idea how to be husbands or wives, much less fathers or mothers.
- Facts versus fake news: Feelings can be enriching or irrational. They are not a reliable source of how we are doing; how we feel is not how we are (or doesn't have to be).
- Not a benevolent dictator: The fact is that emotions determine the destiny of a lot of well-meaning people. Many people let their feelings dictate their attitudes, actions and even identities!
- Not a benevolent judge: Feelings are affected by so many things that there's no way to build anything lasting or meaningful on them. You can't judge the quality of your relationships on your feelings.
- How noble people live: Noble people live from virtues and values, meaning that you train your soul to follow your *will* and not your emotions.
- "Potty training your soul": You simply tell your soul how you are going to behave and how you are going to feel. Then in time, the feelings will follow (not flow out uncontrolled anywhere and everywhere).
- Troubled times: Sometimes our troublesome feelings are telling us the truth about a difficult situation. Yet we still don't let our feelings dictate our responses, because we understand how our choices affect others and ourselves.
- Love is always a choice: Husbands are the ones the Bible specifically exhorts to *love*. Husbands/fathers are tasked with tending the eternal flame that warms the hearts of all of those given into their care.

NINE

Sex and Culture

WHEN A FATHER IS A HEALTHY LOVER, present and engaged, the entire family benefits from his protection and instruction. Mothers and fathers demonstrate romantic love in the context of an eternal covenant, which should fuel conversations that help create a healthy sexual culture at home. In this safe place, fathers and mothers have age-appropriate conversations around sexuality with their kids, which destroys shame, helps inoculate the children from perversion and sometimes even rescues them from the wiles of their own bad choices.

Yet unfortunately, this generation is father deprived, which has left many families uncovered in the radical storms of truthless tales. Countless children find themselves alone, rejected and abandoned, stumbling through the darkness of a loveless existence, looking for hope and starving for connection. This loveless seedbed has created the perfect storm for the weeds of immorality to take root in the hearts of an entire generation. This is fueling a culture of sexual perversion like gasoline on a forest fire. As we discussed earlier, rape, abortion, sex outside marriage, homosexuality, pedophilia and transgenderism have become pandemic in much of the world. But the greatest challenge in this twenty-first-century culture is that we are "normalizing" these perversions! This dynamic is causing the "average" kid to be sucked into the vortex of sexual perversion through the power of suggestion.

Let me illustrate this with a personal story. When Jason, our youngest son, was a preteen, he began completely disconnecting from us. He moped around the house for months like a lost dog on a hot freeway, until one morning I finally got sick of it. I followed him into the laundry room and closed the door behind us. I looked him in the eye and said, "What's going on with you, son?"

Looking away, he replied, "Nothing, Dad. Leave me alone!"

"Sorry, dude, but I am not letting you out of this room until you tell me about the thing I see going on in your eyes!"

"Dad, there's nothing wrong! I'm fine. Really . . . I'm good!"

"Sorry, buddy, but I'm not buying it, and I'm willing to spend the day in the laundry room with you. So it's up to you . . ."

Finally, he blurted out, "*I'm a homosexual!*"

Although I was concerned for Jason, I was also working hard not to laugh. I finally decided to ask the million-dollar question: "Son, what made you decide that you're a homosexual?"

"Dad, another kid and I have been having oral sex with each other," he replied in a quiet voice, staring at the floor.

"So what does that have to do with you being a homosexual, dude?" I shot back in a confident voice.

"I liked it," he said sheepishly.

"Well, son, if you masturbate with your hand and you like it, does that make you a handsexual?" I said in a sarcastic tone.

"No! So having oral sex with him doesn't mean I'm a homosexual?" he asked, peering into my eyes with a sense of relief.

"Nope! It just makes you stupid!" I joked. "Son, all young men make mistakes as they are growing up. They experiment, they fall down and they get back up many times on their journey toward manhood. *It's no big deal!* Wait until you get married and you get to have sex with the woman of your dreams . . . It's going to be ten times better!"

That encounter changed Jason's life forever. What I didn't realize at the time is that it also changed me! Let me take you on a journey while explaining what I mean.

Perversion in the Schools

The truth is, if Jason had grown up without a healthy dad and was exposed to the sexual perversion taught in the public school system today, he might have spent years trying to escape the lie that he was gay. Think about it: Before children begin puberty, they are often only attracted to the same sex. Little girls think boys are gross, and little boys think girls have cooties. Now, consider the powerful effect an influential person like a teacher has on a class of five-year-olds, teaching them that gender is not genetic, but a choice you make. Can you imagine teaching a little girl that she has a vagina, but that she still might be a boy? Or how about telling a young boy that he has a penis, but that he can still choose to be a girl? Talk about mass confusion!

Furthermore, our children are currently being taught (in California, at least) that every sexual preference is healthy, no matter how it affects the family dynamic. Kindergartners, for example, are taught that some "healthy" families have two mommies and no daddy, and other "healthy" families have two daddies and no mommy. Can you imagine the negative impact this is having on the generation of kids who are being taught these fallacies in the public school system?

By the way, parents in California, it has become illegal to pull your kids out of these classes. You probably have figured this out already, but the government has taken over our right and responsibility to raise our kids. They are trying to make us stewards of the government's children! You think I am lying? Do the research.

> **The government has taken over our right and responsibility to raise our kids. They are trying to make us stewards of the government's children!**

Here's the kicker: Christians are raging over the public schools filling their kids' minds with perversion, but they refuse even to talk about sex with their children at home. It's so ironic. It reminds me of the sixties, when the government made prayer in the public school system illegal and Christians protested for months. Yet the surveys in those days showed that few of these protesting parents ever did pray at home with their kids. I guess it's much easier to throw a fit than it is to actually pray!

Sadly, the few American families who do make an effort to educate their kids about sexuality usually reduce their influence down to "The Talk." They typically wait until they think their kids are "old enough" to hear about sex (which is almost always years too late), and then they muster their courage and enter the fray. Red-faced, nervous and embarrassed, they somehow push through the most awkward dialogue they've ever had with any human being. Of course, no matter what words they choose, their demeanor shouts, *Sex is shameful, dirty and disgraceful!* People, this is not the solution.

The Principle of First Mention

Let me describe a powerful dynamic working for (or against) you if you are such a parent. It's called "the principle of first mention." This principle states that whatever you learn *first* about any subject becomes the foundation for the way you *view* that subject for the rest of your life.

For example, if you teach your kids about biblical sexuality first, and later their friend in the sixth grade talks to them about sexual perversion, your kids will measure what their friend said by what you already taught them. In other words, the first one to teach children about any subject is providing them with more than "facts." That person is molding the children's core perspectives and attitudes, handing them the lens that will function like their own private interpreter or tutor on that subject.

On the other hand, if someone else talks to your children about sex before you do, your children will view your opinion through the filter of whatever they were taught first. This will most likely result in them discarding everything you taught them that conflicts with the values the other person shared with them first.

Instead of "The Talk," we need to develop a healthy sexual culture in our homes, in which our children experience the beauty of sexuality against the backdrop of purity. Let me give you an example. Many of our wedding customs in America are rooted in Jewish traditions. Historically, a Jewish wedding lasted seven days. A bridal chamber (which was usually a curtained room with a bed) was erected in the midst of the festival.

After the couple exchanged their vows, they entered the bridal chamber to consummate their covenant, while all the guests waited outside. After the newlyweds had sex for the first time, the groom took the sheet from the bed and hung it over the chamber wall for all the guests to see, displaying the blood from his bride's broken hymen. Then the celebration began. It's important to note here that Jewish weddings were a family affair where kids, teenagers and adults were all in attendance.

> **Instead of "The Talk," we need to develop a healthy sexual culture in our homes, in which our children experience the beauty of sexuality against the backdrop of purity.**

Imagine with me now a little five-year-old boy named Johnny who observes the bloody sheet thrown over the bridal chamber wall, right after he hears all the ruckus in the tent. His first response is probably something like, "Hey, they must have gotten in a fight already!" The bloody sheet, however, serves as a talking point for his parents to introduce an age-appropriate sex talk.

Of course, it's also important to remember that all of this was taking place in the agricultural age, when children were familiar with animals mating on their farms. Society itself was therefore sexually relaxed (not to be confused with immoral) and naturally more holistic. People today are so uptight about sex because the world perverts it and religion shames it. Yet the Kingdom of God should celebrate sex as a gift from the Lord Himself. I mean, orgasms were God's idea. Come on . . . God is good! He could have created us to take turns sitting on an egg for nine months . . . but of course, that would have dramatically reduced the population of the earth.

We Americans are so conditioned to shame sex that we unconsciously do it to our children. I often cringe at the way parents teach their kids to name their own body parts. It usually goes something like this:

"Molly, this is your nose. Say *nooose*."
"Nooose!"

125

"That's so good, Molly. Now touch your ears . . . say *earrrs*."

"Earrrs!"

"Okay, Molly, now touch your mouth . . . say *mouthhh*."

"Mouthhh!"

"Very good. . . . Oh no, Molly, don't play with your dinky! That's bad!"

Calling a vagina, a penis or breasts by silly names communicates shame, guilt, disgrace and dishonor to our children. Furthermore, children naturally discover their own bodies by putting their fingers in their ears, pulling on their tongue and touching their penis or vagina. Parents often panic at this, thinking their small children are masturbating or fearing that their kids might have been molested. Of course, in this perverted world we live in, anything is possible. But the truth is that most often, this self-exploration is just the healthy way in which small children discover their own bodies.

Watch and Wait

Have you ever watched a commercial for a drug on TV, and just before it concludes, like a machine gun in a video game, suddenly some guy rattles off a ton of possible side effects? Some of the side effects are so ridiculously bad that they're hilarious (unless, of course, you are taking the drug). One terrifying example is an ad I saw for the antidepressant Prozac. The commercial begins with a woman running through a field of flowers as a soothing voice talks about the benefits of Prozac . . . how it helps thousands of people live active, anxiety-free lives.

Then suddenly the announcer's voice speeds up drastically, and the guy begins rattling off all the dreadful side effects of the medication. "Don't take this drug if you are dah . . . dah . . . dah. Prozac may cause self-destructive thoughts, and in some cases may result in suicide, violent tendencies, deep depression, extreme anxiety . . . etc."

What?! a viewer thinks. *I thought I was being prescribed the drug to help with my depression, and now you're telling me it might encourage me to kill myself? Hello! How do I know if I'm one of those poor, unlucky suckers? Yikes!*

This Prozac commercial reminds me so much of the politically correct society we live in, where the side effects of our cultural solutions are often many times worse than the problems we are endeavoring to cure. Consequently, many bad laws are passed to deal with an isolated incident or a small percentage of the population. Often, those laws have terribly negative side effects on the rest of the world. The entire pro-choice movement, for example, was established on back alley abortions and terrible science. Stories of women dying in dark alleys, bleeding to death by self-induced abortions, were dramatized in the highest court of our land. Consequently, it opened the floodgates to the genocide of 1.5 million infants a year in America alone.

Abortion on demand is part of a deeply rooted, devious plot. Here is my case: The highest percentage of abortions are performed on black women.[1] The irony of the situation is not lost when you consider that Planned Parenthood founder, Margaret Sanger—once reported as stating that "negros are human weeds that should be exterminated"—placed her first "Women's Health Clinic" (which consequently performed abortions) in Harlem, a black ghetto in Chicago. In fact, during the rise of the Black Lives Matter movement in 2020, Planned Parenthood actually disavowed Sanger because it has now been proven that she was a racist.[2] If Sanger was a racist who hated black people, then why would she put her first "health clinic" in an all-black neighborhood? It certainly wasn't to help black women! It was then, and continues to be now, an abortion mill disguised as a health clinic, with a goal of participating in the "extermination of the human weeds." The sad thing is that although Margaret Sanger died in 1966, the same evil scenario continues to this day, and with growing momentum.

Then there was Norma McCorvey, who was "Roe" in the infamous case of *Roe v. Wade*. She was the woman who petitioned the Supreme Court to

> **Many bad laws are passed to deal with an isolated incident or a small percentage of the population. Often, those laws have terribly negative side effects on the rest of the world.**

legalize abortion in America. McCorvey spent the rest of her life, however, as a pro-life woman fighting the very law she helped to pass.

A couple of years ago, one of my students challenged me on my transgender position. He said, "My friend pointed out to me that there are people who are called hermaphrodites, and they're born with both male and female genitalia." He therefore concluded that transgenderism must be normal.

"There are also people born with no arms and/or legs. Would you say this is normal?" I responded. "Why would you redefine the entire population of the earth simply because a very small percentage of people are born with a deformity? Sometimes in our need to help a person who is struggling with a unique condition feel better about the circumstances or situation, we *abnormalize* an entire culture to try to normalize the person's condition," I continued. "The truth is that the worst laws, philosophies and theological ideas are often developed in reaction to a few people's pain."

Looking quite dumbfounded, the young man replied, "I never thought of it that way."

He was right. He had never thought of it that way before because we live in an immoral culture in which people are always trying to justify their sin on the altar of humanism.

The Church Is Absent

Where does the Church stand on all of this? I would propose that we historically stand on the sidelines of culture, screaming at the players, watching the reruns of the game on the six o'clock news, but we rarely get in the game. It's just too messy, and we certainly don't want to offend anyone. In fact, if you are offended by this book, it might be because no church leader has ever talked to you so openly and blatantly about sex.

A case in point: In 2018, California was trying to pass some more very radical transgender laws that would have a dramatic negative effect on the children of our state. The good news is that those political actions began waking Christians up to the fact that our silence has left society in the hands of perverts who have hijacked our government and are destroying our families. Our church decided to take a stand and finally do something to stop the perversion. Our Senior Leadership Team met and talked for hours about an effective strategy that could lead to changing the hearts and minds in society. At one point in the meeting, we decided to teach about homosexuality and transgenderism in a Sunday morning service. It was a bold step for our team. But a week later, in a follow-up meeting, we realized that we couldn't speak on homosexuality because we have *never* spoken a single message on healthy sexuality in the sixty years of Bethel Church's history! Teaching on homosexuality and transgenderism would therefore feel like an unwise reaction to the LGBTQ agenda, not like a holistic approach to shepherding our people. Yet maybe the greatest revelation of our leadership gathering was the fact that we were a big part of the problem. Although the Bible talks about sex from Genesis to Revelation, we had never taught our congregation about God's perspective on sexuality.

I'm proud to say that we have taken some bold steps forward as a church since then. We have developed classes, written books and built curriculum on the subject of healthy sexuality for both leaders and our congregation. Our teams also have built a very compassionate ministry to the gay community, which is led by Elizabeth Woning and Ken Williams, who were both formerly gay. Their ministry is called Equipped to Love, and they lead a movement called CHANGED, which is a coalition of hundreds of once-gay people who have banded together to give hope to others who want to be free from homosexuality. We also started a ministry called Moral Revolution (in addition to writing a book by the same name back in 2012), to inspire a healthy sexual reformation all over the world.

This is a good start, but the real work has just begun. Ultimately, holistic societies can only be built on healthy families. Churches tend to build orphanages to deal with this fatherless pandemic, which is better than homeless children, but it is a far cry from a real family. We *must* become the hands and heart of our heavenly Father to a prodigal generation whose members have squandered their inheritance, trampled on their legacy and lost their identity.

EPIC
TAKEAWAYS

- When dads are healthy lovers: Then mothers and fathers demonstrate romantic love in the context of an eternal covenant, which should fuel conversations that help create a healthy sexual culture at home.

- When dads are absent: Then families are uncovered in the radical storms of truthless tales being told to them by a politically correct but perverse culture.

- Unsafe schools: Our children are currently being taught (in California, at least) that every sexual preference is healthy, no matter how it affects the family dynamic. Can you imagine the negative impact this fallacy is having on this generation of kids?

- The principle of first mention: This principle states that whatever you learn *first* about any subject becomes the foundation for the way you *view* that subject for the rest of your life. That's why parents must be the *first* ones to talk to their children about sexuality!

- Compounding the problem: In the politically correct society in which we live, the side effects of our cultural solutions are often many times worse than the problems we are endeavoring to cure. The entire pro-choice movement and its resulting genocide of infants is one example.

- Absent Christians, wake up: The Church's silence has left society in the hands of perverts who have hijacked our government and are destroying our families. We need to take a stand and do something about it.

- How to build healthy: Holistic societies can only be built on healthy families. We *must* become the hands and heart of our heavenly Father to a prodigal generation.

TEN

Bonded in Battle

PERVERSION IS SO PREVALENT IN OUR CULTURE TODAY that the line between love and sex has become blurred, or even nonexistent. Consequently, many people have misunderstood their God-given need to have healthy, bonded relationships with both men and women. The importance of such relationships is illustrated beautifully in the life of David, the man after God's heart. Let's jump into one of the most epic stories ever inked and see what we can learn from this famous warrior/king.

David killed Goliath and delivered the Israelites from their archenemy, the Philistines. His courage and victory catapulted him to overnight fame. In fact, so great was his victory that when the Israeli army returned home, the city put on a parade to welcome the men back. The women lined the streets of Jerusalem and sang, "Saul has slain his thousands, and David his ten thousands" (1 Samuel 18:7). Suffice it to say here that the song wasn't on King Saul's Top 40 hits list (more on that later). Yet there was another powerful subplot going on behind the scenes in the palace. The king's son Jonathan, who himself was a great warrior and was the rightful heir to the throne, bonded with David on the battlefield. The Bible puts it like this: "The soul of Jonathan was knit to the soul of David, and Jonathan loved him as himself" (1 Samuel 18:1).

At first, King Saul was excited about their friendship and refused to let David go home to his family. Then story intensifies when "Jonathan made a covenant with David because he loved him as himself. Jonathan stripped himself of the robe that was on him and gave it to David, with his armor, including his sword and his bow and his belt" (verses 3–4). I'm not sure if you get what happened here, but the robe wasn't simply Jon's favorite coat; it was actually his royal apparel. He basically had just knighted David as heir to the throne in his place! But Jonathan wasn't done. This radical revolutionary took off his armor and gave it to David, and then surrendered his weapons to the guy. To become this vulnerable to a warrior kid from the other side of the tracks, Jonathan was either crazy or incredibly anointed.

What Jonathan didn't know was that Samuel, the most famous prophet and judge in all of Israel, had already commissioned David a few months earlier to become king in place of Jon's father, Saul. So the plot thickens! But the real question here is, *Why?* Why did a rich and famous dude who had it all lay it all down for another guy? The answer is simple . . . well, kind of simple, but really, deeply profound: Jonathan loved David as he loved himself. He so loved David that he made a covenant with him, meaning he laid

> Love changes the rules, flips the script and transcends logic and reason.

down his life for him. *Crazy*, you say? Maybe, but love changes the rules, flips the script and transcends logic and reason.

Unfortunately, the story gets ugly after this. King Saul couldn't bring himself to celebrate the teenage warrior's success. Instead, he took the stupid road and became jealous of David (who was making the king look like a genius). Saul was so crazed with envy, and was bound by so much suspicion, that he became possessed by a murdering, evil spirit. (You can't make this stuff up!) Saul lost his mind and became obsessed with killing David. For fourteen years, the madman king, along with the entire Israeli army, pursued young David through the wilderness and from city to city, killing anyone who helped David. So irrational was Saul's murdering spree that he literally gave the order for 85 Levitical priests, their wives, their children and even their infants to be hacked up with a sword, probably forcing their family members to watch as they waited their turn (see 1 Samuel 22:11–23).

Miraculously, David, with a small band of brothers numbering about four hundred men, managed to escape over and over again. As you can imagine, King Saul's killing spree and desperate pursuit of David tested Jonathan's covenant with his friend. Jon was constantly pulled between his love for David and his loyalty to his father. Yet he continually renewed his covenant of friendship with David, had secret meetings with him and worked hard to protect his friend by feeding him intel concerning Saul's plots. But at the end of the day, it wasn't David who died at the hand of Saul; it was Jonathan and Saul who fell in battle, ironically against the Philistines whom David had defeated a decade earlier.

When a young carrier brought David the news of Saul's and Jonathan's deaths, David ripped his clothes and lamented in a song, "How have the mighty fallen in the midst of the battle! Jonathan is slain on your high places. I am distressed for you, my brother Jonathan; you have been very pleasant to me. Your love to me was more wonderful than the love of women. How have the mighty fallen" (2 Samuel 1:25–27). This isn't some secret homosexual relationship, exposed in a weak moment of a lover's loss, as some have alleged. No! This is a warrior's lamentation over his fallen brother—two men who bonded in battle and who grew in love for one another. What is unearthed by these covenant brothers is the fact that healthy men need other healthy men in their lives.

It's true that God created men with a sexual desire and the need to bond with a wife (although some men are called to be single). A wife completes her husband (and a husband completes his wife) in a way that is supernatural. Nothing should ever interfere, replace or compete with the bond of marriage, except for God Himself. Marriage is the highest level of covenant, in which two people become one flesh. Therefore, as husbands we *must never* let anything or anyone siphon off our need for our wives, or our affection for them.

Yet there is an essential desire in every man that can't be satisfied by a woman. It's a desire deeply rooted in the very DNA of every man, and it manifests in a longing to foster deep connections with other men. There are a variety of ways that this need is fulfilled in different men at various seasons of their lives. Some of the most common expressions of this are brother to brother, father to son, mentor to mentee, discipler to disciple, friend to friend and so forth. In fact, healthy guys often have a few different men who meet a variety of needs in their lives. It's common for a healthy man to have a father figure (whether biological, spiritual or both), while also bonding with brothers (biological, spiritual or both) and friends (peer to peer). Furthermore, a man may be discipling another brother at the same time as he fosters these relationships for himself.

David's Mighty Men

David had a brother-to-brother relationship with Jonathan that was birthed on the battlefield and fostered in the palace as a friendship. Or more accurately, they were comrades in a covenant relationship in which they vowed their lives to one another. I think it's so common for men who fight together in war, protecting each other in foxholes and risking their lives for one another, to bond so deeply that they become nearly inseparable.

Of course, Jonathan's position as heir to the throne, and David as the man after God's heart, who was commissioned to be the next king of Israel in place of Jon's father, Saul, certainly created a powerful yet complex narrative in their relationship. This narrative was likely the catalyst for the incredibly moving vow that Jonathan had made to David, which virtually guaranteed his friend the throne. Yet David also had a host of other men who saw him as a father/leader (not a peer), but who were equally as bonded with him as Jonathan was. David encountered many of these men when he was a fugitive running for his life from King Saul. Here is David's first introduction to those who would become "the mighty men of David":

> So David departed from there and escaped to the cave of Adullam; and when his brothers and all his father's household heard of it, they went down there to him. Everyone who was in distress, and everyone who was in debt, and everyone who was discontented gathered to him; and he became captain over them. Now there were about four hundred men with him.
>
> 1 Samuel 22:1–2

David's relationship with his men is so intriguing and complex that it literally could be a book in itself. David was a noble man who had loved God from his youth. Yet unlike most people, who attract others like themselves, David didn't attract *who he was*; he attracted *whom he loved*. Consequently, his "band of brothers," so to speak, were a bunch of discontent, disgruntled, societal rejects whom nobody else wanted. And David had a profound effect on the hearts of these men, who followed him for much of their lives.

One of the most telling signs of David's influence on these men's lives was the fact that he was a giant-killer and his men became giant-killers themselves. In fact, when David grew old, he went after the four brothers of Goliath, confronting them on a battlefield. The fight escalated into a fierce battle in which David was nearly killed. But David's men jumped into the fight and rescued him from the giants' grasp, killing the four giants in the process. It's epic to me that it was David's band of warriors who eradicated the giants—the very force that had kept the Israelites out of their Promised Land—and purged the land of those evil predators once and for all (see 2 Samuel 21:18–22).

> **One of the most telling signs of David's influence on these men's lives was the fact that he was a giant-killer and his men became giant-killers themselves.**

Yet the story of David and his mighty men goes so much deeper than just a bunch of tough guys who terrorized Israel's enemies. These men became noble, devoted lovers of God themselves. Their loyalty to David saved what historians call "the golden years of Israel."

You might be asking yourself, *Why is he telling me about David and his men?*

I'm sharing their stories with you because I see so many principles in their relationships that we can apply to our own lives. Furthermore, I'm convinced that many men feel lost or unprepared for the treacherous jungle we call life because they have never bonded with a brother or a father themselves. This is reinforced by the very fact that Jesus never called His followers *Christians*; instead, He always referred to them as *disciples*. The obvious connotation is that there was someone *discipling* them.

> I'm convinced that many men feel lost or unprepared for the treacherous jungle we call life because they have never bonded with a brother or a father themselves.

Think about it: If I am called a *son*, it means I must have a mother and/or a father. If am referred to as an *employee*, then there must be an employer. If I am a *husband*, then, of course, there must be a wife . . . you get the idea. The very title *disciple* implies or even demands a specific kind of relationship with someone else. There have been many leaders over the last century, however, who have taught the principles of discipleship without understanding the need for men to bond with other men the way the disciples bonded with Jesus and one another. (Women also need other women in the same way.)

It's also important to understand that David wasn't a glorified gang leader who became a king. In fact, he refused to take part in any coup to overthrow the throne. One of the most stunning displays of loyalty ever experienced in the history of the world has to be David's unwavering devotion to King Saul. Despite Saul losing his mind and becoming a paranoid, schizophrenic, murdering psychopath, David refused to kill him or even defend himself against him. The pinnacle of David's fierce loyalty was on full display one afternoon when he and his men were hiding deep inside a cave, trying to avoid Saul's wrath. Saul entered the cave to take a crap, completely unaware of the situation. With Saul squatted in the most vulnerable position, David's men begged him to let them kill him, even citing a prophetic word God had given David. Check out their dialogue:

> The men of David said to him, "Behold, this is the day of which the Lord said to you, 'Behold; I am about to give your enemy into your hand, and you shall do to him as it seems good to you.'" Then David arose and cut off the edge of Saul's robe secretly. It came about afterward that David's

conscience bothered him because he had cut off the edge of Saul's robe. So he said to his men, "Far be it from me because of the LORD that I should do this thing to my lord, the LORD's anointed, to stretch out my hand against him, since he is the LORD's anointed." David persuaded his men with these words and did not allow them to rise up against Saul. And Saul arose, left the cave, and went on his way.

1 Samuel 24:4–7

This is radical loyalty, but it's not the end of this wild story. David waited until Saul was a safe distance away and then exited the cave himself, shouting at King Saul to check the edge of his robe. When Saul realized a piece of his robe was missing, and he saw David waving it like a flag from the cave, the king was wrecked with grief! He repented to David and headed home. Unfortunately, the king was so demonized and unstable that rage soon overtook him again. A few months later, Saul, again full of rage, pursued David like a man on fire. This time, David and his men were hiding in the mountains when they observed Saul and his entire army asleep in a valley below. Here is the account of the situation, according to Samuel:

David and Abishai came to the people by night, and behold, Saul lay sleeping inside the circle of the camp with his spear stuck in the ground at his head; and Abner and the people were lying around him. Then Abishai said to David, "Today God has delivered your enemy into your hand; now therefore, please let me strike him with the spear to the ground with one stroke, and I will not strike him the second time." But David said to Abishai, "Do not destroy him, for who can stretch out his hand against the LORD's anointed and be without guilt? . . . The LORD forbid that I should stretch out my hand against the LORD's anointed; but now please take the spear that is at his head and the jug of water, and let us go." So David took the spear and the jug of water from beside Saul's head, and they went away, but no one saw or knew it, nor did any awake, for they were all asleep, because a sound sleep from the LORD had fallen on them.

1 Samuel 26:7–9, 11–12

When the day dawned, David called out to Abner, King Saul's personal bodyguard, and taunted him for being asleep on the job. He basically said, "Yo, dude! Some mighty man you are, letting enemies have full access to the king while you slept. Look, I have your spear and your jug of water. You failed! You and all the king's army deserve to die!" Again, King Saul repented, telling David that he had played the fool and made a serious mistake about him. (You think?) And I already spilled the beans on the end of this story. Soon after this last incident, King Saul and his son Jonathan died in battle.

Royal Lessons in Nobility and Loyalty

Over the next forty years, many more men joined David as he became king of Israel, and they went on to eradicate Israel's enemies in battle. But those first 400 broken men who bonded with David on the battlefield and laid their lives down for him ultimately became a famous, noble and godly military force feared by all the surrounding nations. Those men literally took on the noble characteristics of their leader.

King David assigned 33 of these 400 men the title of "the mighty men of David." These 33 men would make the Green Berets look like a Boy Scout troop. They were so fierce on the battlefield that one of them named Josheb-basshebeth killed 800 enemy soldiers by himself (see 2 Samuel 23:8). Another guy named Abishai killed 300 enemy soldiers in one battle by himself (see verses 18–19). And get this—he wasn't even among the top three toughest guys on David's force. Another guy named Benaiah saw a lion fall into a pit on a snowy day and jumped down into the pit and killed it with a sword, not to mention the many other outrageous acts of bravery he accomplished (see verses 20–22).

> Those first 400 broken men who bonded with David on the battlefield and laid their lives down for him ultimately became a famous, noble and godly military force feared by all the surrounding nations.

These mighty men proved their loyalty to David over and over. Yet the greatest test of loyalty for them actually took place in the twilight years of King David's life, when he was so sick that they could barely keep him alive. Let me explain. Although God and David had promised Solomon (David and Bathsheba's son) the throne, Adonijah (another of David's sons from a different wife) rebelled against his father, incited a coup and pronounced himself king of Israel. The most challenging aspect of the coup was that Adonijah had won over Joab, who was in charge of the Israeli army. He had also gained favor with most of the religious leaders and the Who's Who of Israel. So Adonijah threw an inauguration party for himself, which almost all of Israel attended. Yet Zadok the priest, Nathan the prophet, Benaiah (the guy who killed the lion in the pit) and "the mighty men who belonged to David" were not with Adonijah (see 1 Kings 1:5–8). These men had learned loyalty years before by watching David honor King Saul during Saul's murderous rampage. Now, although the odds were stacked against them, they refused to follow the crowd to Adonijah. In fact, they were so famous for their loyalty to David that the Bible says Adonijah "did not invite Nathan the prophet, Benaiah, the mighty men, and Solomon his brother" to his celebration (1 Kings 1:10).

When the prophet Nathan, and Bathsheba, David's wife, found out about the insurrection, they strategically went to David and communicated the situation to him. David immediately ordered Solomon to be placed on the king's donkey and ushered to the throne, protected by Benaiah and the mighty men. When this procession arrived at Gihon, they anointed Solomon as king there and blew trumpets, proclaiming, "Long live King Solomon!" (verse 34).

This proclamation ruined Adonijah's party. Joab, the commander of the Israeli army, freaked out in fear of Solomon and the mighty men of David. He took off running for his life! The Bible goes on to say that "all the guests of Adonijah were terrified; and they arose and each went on his way" (verse 49). When the smoke cleared, Joab and Adonijah were put to death for their rebellion, and "the golden years of Israel" were preserved in King Solomon.

Disciples

I want you to know that God is still taking broken men and transforming them into history makers and world changers! And although we don't live in the Old Testament anymore, and therefore we don't measure mighty men by how many enemy soldiers they kill in one battle, it is still true that we are in a spiritual battle for the very soul of our nations.

> **God is still taking broken men and transforming them into history makers and world changers!**

Furthermore, God is empowering His disciples, as soldiers of the Kingdom, to destroy the works of darkness and bring His light to a dark and decrepit world. Much like David's mighty men, these disciples must also be trained, equipped and deployed by leaders who can model nobility, loyalty and honor as they bond together in battle. There is no one in the New Testament who models this more profoundly than the apostle Paul. He discipled many men, some of whom became his spiritual sons. Here is a short excerpt from a letter Paul wrote to one of his spiritual sons named Timothy:

> You therefore, my son, be strong in the grace that is in Christ Jesus. The things which you have heard from me in the presence of many witnesses, entrust these to faithful men who will be able to teach others also. Suffer hardship with me, as a good soldier of Christ Jesus. No soldier in active service entangles himself in the affairs of everyday life, so that he may please the one who enlisted him as a soldier.
>
> 2 Timothy 2:1–4

The similarities between David's relationship with his mighty men and what we glean from the relationship Paul had with his men are stunning. Paul and Timothy, for example, weren't two friends hanging out together at church. No! These were comrades who bonded on a different kind of battlefield than David's men did, yet it was a battlefield no less dangerous and no less significant.

The truth is that all of us have an inner longing to belong, to be cared about and to be loved—to know we are wanted (not just needed), and to be understood and celebrated. King David was so bonded with his special force of mighty men that the Bible follows David's very last words with a list of these men one by one. "These are the last words of King David," 2 Samuel 23 begins, and then gives his final words in verses 1–7. The very next verse begins, "These are the names of the mighty men whom David had . . ." (see verses 8–39). It then lists the names of all his mighty men and gives highlights of their exploits. It's epic to me that the most famous king in the entire Bible, the guy who wrote most of the psalms, seemed to be thinking about his mighty men on his death bed!

The last thing I want to point out before we leave this chapter is that the Bible says, "These are the men whom David *had*" (2 Samuel 23:8, emphasis added). These men *belonged* to David. They weren't just enlisted soldiers or casual friends; they were *his* men! I know a statement like this can be dangerous or even sound cultlike to some, but the truth is that we were born to be connected, to belong somewhere and to be bonded to our people.

EPIC
TAKEAWAYS

- Relationships are important: Because of the blurry line between love and sex in today's perverse culture, many people misunderstand their God-given need to have healthy bonded relationships with both men and women.
- Covenant brothers: The strong bond between David and Jonathan, birthed on the battlefield, shows how healthy men need other healthy men in their lives.
- Nobility begets nobility: David was a noble man who had loved God from his youth. Because of his profound effect on his ragtag band of four hundred followers, they became noble, devoted lovers of God themselves.
- The pinnacle of loyalty: Loyal to God first and foremost, David refused to harm King Saul, the Lord's anointed, even though the king was determined to harm him. David lived out loyalty in front of his men, and they, in turn, were fiercely loyal to him, right up to the end of his life.
- Transformation still happens: God is still taking broken men and transforming them into history makers and world changers!
- Empowered to impact others: God is empowering His disciples, as soldiers of the Kingdom, to destroy the works of darkness and bring His light to a dark and decrepit world.
- Born to bond together: The truth is that we were born to be connected, to belong somewhere and to be bonded to our people.

ELEVEN

The Art of Discipleship

ALTHOUGH I LOVE DAVID'S STORY, I struggled to bond with anyone personally, especially men. I think it's because I grew up in a very abusive home. My father drowned when I was three years young, and my mother remarried twice. My mom was an amazing woman, but after my father's death she began looking for love in all the wrong places. Consequently, both my stepfathers were very broken, angry and violent abusers. I could go into all the gory details, but it will suffice to say here that I was beaten on many occasions, while my mother physically tried to protect me and my two siblings from these men. I moved out of the house at seventeen with a broken heart and a crushed spirit. To say I was "damaged goods" would be an understatement, but I am a fighter, and I was determined to shake off seventeen years of bondage and find my Promised Land.

My mom divorced my first stepfather when I was about thirteen, and another intense drama commenced in our lives. We suddenly had a prowler at our house nearly every night for an entire year. The police patrolled around our house continually, while my mother slept on the couch with a shotgun and I slept in my bed with a .22-caliber rifle. Despite all the security, the guy got into our house twice. The second time, he entered through my bedroom window. That night, I woke up and started shouting at the prowler. He jumped out the window as I quickly grabbed my rifle and took a shot at him, thankfully missing him. Consequently, the stress of all the craziness caused psoriasis to break out over most of my mother's body. Personally, I was terrified, and although I was trying to be the man of the house, I could barely function.

> **Personally, I was terrified, and although I was trying to be the man of the house, I could barely function.**

The night after the prowler broke into my bedroom, I couldn't sleep. I wasn't raised to believe in God, but I was desperate for help. So I sat up in my bed and said out loud, *If there is a God, and if You heal my mother, I will find out who You are and serve You the rest of my life.*

An audible voice answered back, *My name is Jesus Christ, and you have what you requested!*

The next morning, the psoriasis was gone from my mother's body. And a couple of days later, the police caught the prowler. I was rocked . . . I mean, completely wrecked!

About a week later, I was lying in my bed late at night and the audible voice spoke to me again. He said, *My name is Jesus Christ, and you said if I healed your mother, you would serve Me. I am waiting!*

The Search

I spent the next three years on a desperate search for the God who spoke to me that night. My journey led me in and out of several churches while I tried to discern whether or not the God who spoke to me was in the building. Frankly, I didn't have much to go on because I could hardly read, and therefore the Scriptures were a complete mystery to me. He had said His name was Jesus Christ, so that at least eliminated Buddhism and the Muslim faith from the list. I also raised my hand four different times to receive Christ and repeat a prayer over those three years, but nothing changed in my life at all.

By the second year of my search, my girlfriend, Kathy (who later became my wife), joined me on the search-and-rescue team to find the God who had spoken to me. Three long years passed as we passionately pursued the Voice.

Finally, something profound happened. We were invited to a "Jesus People" meeting in a couple's home on a Wednesday night. We arrived there early and sat on the front-room floor, but within minutes the place was jam-packed with hippie kids. They were everywhere, including on the front lawn.

A few minutes later, the worship began, and the place was electric with faith. As we worshiped, young people stood up spontaneously one by one to share short testimonies: "God healed me from cancer . . . ," "God delivered me from heroin . . . ," God healed my epilepsy . . . ," "Jesus delivered me from demons . . ." On and on it went, for more than an hour.

Finding Fathers

When the worship was over, the young worship leader asked, "Does anyone want to become a disciple of Jesus?" Kathy and I both raised our hands and prayed a simple prayer (as I had done four times before). But what floored me is what happened an hour later. The leader came over and joined us on the floor. Then he pulled out his Bible and explained salvation to us in very simple terms. He taught us that we were now "born again," and that we were like spiritual children who needed a father. A few minutes later, he called two young men over, and they plopped down on the floor next to us. He said, "Which one of these men do you want to be your spiritual father?"

I just picked the better-looking one, named Art Kipperman, and that day he became our father. Art was only four years older than I was (he was 22, and I was 18). But he was much wiser, especially in the things of God. Art was a quiet, simple man, but he changed our lives. Kathy and I met with him every week for three years. When Art got married, his wife became part of our leadership team, and they discipled us like Holy Spirit life coaches.

> The leader taught us that we were now "born again," and that we were like spiritual children who needed a father.

I had a nervous breakdown at the end of the third year that Art was discipling us. Hoping I could get well, Kathy and I moved to a small town called Lewiston, in the Trinity Alps of Northern California. This is the town I told you about in the opening chapter, where our gym experiences with the fatherless kids later took place. Moving away from Art was devastating for me; I truly didn't know what I had until it was gone. I was in the midst of the hardest time of my life, and I was three hundred miles away from my spiritual father. Remember, this was all before cell phones and Zoom calls, so I was a mess.

I prayed every day that God would send me a new spiritual father to take Art's place. About a year passed, and I was working as a mechanic in a repair shop in town. One day, I was lying on a creeper underneath a green Jeep Wagoneer, crying and asking God to "send me a father." Suddenly, I heard the Lord tell me, *The man who owns this Jeep will be your father!* The Voice was so clear that it stunned me.

I had never met the owner of the Jeep, but I was hoping he was at least a Christian. At the end of the day, the customer finally came in to pick up his vehicle. I was so nervous I could hardly talk! He was a tall, balding guy about twenty years older than me. The first thing I noticed was that he was so kind and joyful, and love oozed out of him. I explained the work order to him, took his money and walked him out to his Jeep. We said our good-byes as he got in his rig to leave. As soon as he started his car, I panicked. *Oh no! I'm never going to see him again*, I thought to myself. I leaned over and knocked on his side window. He rolled down the window and smiled as he waited for me to gather myself. I felt like an orphan, waiting to be adopted. With tears streaming down my face, I blurted out, "God told me that the man who owns this Jeep will be my father! Are you a Christian?"

"Yes," he exclaimed with a big smile. He turned off the motor, opened the door and climbed out of his rig, with his arms wide open. He hugged me and said, "I would be honored to be your spiritual father!"

The man's name is Bill Derryberry, and he has been a father to me for four decades. He is an anchor in my worst storms, a voice of reason in my most important decisions and an angel on my shoulder who has inspired, encouraged and celebrated me most of my adult life.

Why? Why? Why?

The challenge is that many of us were raised in a global orphanage of isolation because our fathers were either disconnected, abusive or nonexistent, leaving us to fend for ourselves. Furthermore, most of us don't trust authority figures because they didn't use their position to protect, provide for and promote us. Instead, we were controlled, abused and abandoned. So the question we ask is, *Why? Why* do I need to be discipled? *Why* do I need a father in my life? *Why* can't I do life by myself?

The answer to these questions is simple yet complex. The simple answer is that God designed you to be interdependent, not independent. If you are male, you were born to be bonded to other men, celebrated, instructed by leaders and connected to a band of brothers. If you are female, you were created to be bonded to other women.

> The challenge is that many of us were raised in a global orphanage of isolation because our fathers were either disconnected, abusive or nonexistent, leaving us to fend for ourselves.

As I pointed out in the previous chapter, the apostle Paul had a father-son relationship with Timothy. Their relationship was close, but it was never meant to be exclusive. The truth is that their relationship was supposed to be a model for the churches that Paul was overseeing. Examine this dialogue Paul had with the Corinthian brothers and sisters:

> I do not write these things to shame you, but to admonish you as my beloved children. For if you were to have countless tutors [teachers] in Christ, yet you would not have many fathers, for in Christ Jesus I became your father through the gospel. Therefore I exhort you, be imitators of me. For this reason I have sent to you Timothy, who is my beloved and faithful child in the Lord, and he will remind you of my ways which are in Christ, just as I teach everywhere in every church.
>
> 1 Corinthians 4:14–17

Paul was explaining to these new Greek converts that he was not just their teacher, but their father in the faith. The distinction he made here is that teachers or tutors give us necessary instruction, but fathers are role models we should imitate. In other words, instructors teach what they know, but fathers impart who they are! This reminds me of the African elephant story I shared with you in chapter 4. Remember how the adult male elephants modeled for the younger males how to manage their aggression, and how the young male elephants became violent in the absence of their fathers? Those young elephants needed role models to imitate so they could learn to be "elephant-like."

The Corinthians were first-generation believers who had just come out of Greek mythology, which was full of sexual perversion, polygamy, homosexuality and pedophilia. Several Christian teachers were instructing these first-century believers. Yet Paul had a deep concern that the Corinthian church would exchange (or confuse) teachers with fathers, so he sent them one of his spiritual sons, Timothy. What was Tim's assignment? Model sonship for this church that desperately needed fathers. Paul didn't send them a powerful teacher who could give them deep revelation about discipleship, nor did he commission a prophet to foretell their divine family's future. No! He sent them a loyal, loving son so they could observe Timothy's relationship to his spiritual father (Paul) and receive the impartation of the grace they needed to shift their lives from bastards to sons. (We'll look at this shift more closely in a moment, when we look at Hebrews 12.)

I like to describe Paul's relationship with the Corinthians as tough love, as he sometimes hit them over the head with a two-by-four to get their attention. Look at the dialogue he has with them just a few verses after letting them know he was their father:

> Now some have become arrogant, as though I were not coming to you. But I will come to you soon, if the Lord wills, and I shall find out, not the words of those who are arrogant but their power. For the kingdom of God does not consist in words but in power. What do you desire? Shall I come to you with a rod, or with love and a spirit of gentleness?
>
> 1 Corinthians 4:18–21

Discipling believers who are coming out of a cult is no cakewalk, but Paul is up to the task. He is direct, honest and even fierce when he feels it is necessary. This passage of Scripture reminds me of one of my first conflicts with Bill Derryberry. He called my house to see how I was doing one day, but I wasn't home. He asked Kathy, "Where did Kris go?"

"Kris went to Redding to buy a Jeep," she responded.

"A Jeep?!" he grumbled. "You guys need a new car like you need a hole in the head. You guys can't hardly pay the bills you have now!"

Bill was right, and what he learned about me that day was that whenever I felt down or low, I would go spend money to make myself feel better. The worse I felt, the larger the purchase I would make. This was my life pattern.

I had just arrived at the Jeep dealership in Redding, an hour's drive from our home, and was scoping out the cars on the lot when the loudspeaker proclaimed, "*Kris Vallotton to the sales desk . . . you have a phone call!*"

I panicked. Kathy was the only one who knew I was at the dealership, and I imagined the worst. I ran across the lot, and completely out of breath, I answered the phone. "Hello?" I said anxiously.

Without a greeting, a voice shouted, "*What are you doing looking at Jeeps?*" Before I could answer, it continued, "*Get your butt home now!*"

You guessed it—it was Bill. And he was furious that I could be so irresponsible. Bill was almost always very mild-mannered, but he also had a way of giving you a good butt kicking when necessary. In fact, Bill took me "out to the woodshed" several times in the early years of our relationship. But he was always so forgiving and loving to me that it never felt controlling or abusive.

Kathy also has a relationship with Bill. In the early days of our marriage, she would often call him and let him know that I was being a butthead at home. Bill and I had lunch together every week, and I could always tell when I was in trouble because he would open our conversation by asking me how things were going at home. Bill isn't a deeply philosophical marriage counselor; he's more of an encourager who exemplifies love for his own wife and children. He often would exhort me, "Lay down your life for Kathy. Take on a servant's heart and stop trying to be right."

Bill is incredibly kind, honest and transparent. I always leave his presence feeling loved and valued, even when he corrects me. Bill is in his late eighties now, and our roles have changed. He is still my biggest fan, but it's my turn to be the encourager, the lover and the listener in his life.

Tell Me the Truth

There is so much abuse in the Body of Christ that I hesitate to share this, but men need fathers and leaders who love them enough to confront them, and who are wise enough to know when the time is right. Of course, being controlling, harsh or rude is an elder-brother style of leadership, which is dysfunctional and unhealthy.

All believers need encouragement, love and instruction, but they also need discipline. Many twenty-first-century Christians are so rebellious that they won't submit to anyone. Because they have an orphan mindset, they don't know how to be sons. When you correct them, they commonly play the victim card and disappear for weeks.

The Hebrews writer had a ton to say about this subject. He wrote,

> "My son, do not regard lightly the discipline of the LORD, nor faint when you are reproved by Him; for those whom the LORD loves He disciplines, and He scourges every son whom he receives."
>
> It is for discipline that you endure; God deals with you as with sons; for what son is there whom his father does not discipline? But if you are without discipline, of which all have become partakers, then you are illegitimate children [bastards] and not sons. Furthermore, we had earthly fathers to discipline us, and we respected them; shall we not much rather be subject to the Father of spirits, and live? For they disciplined us for a short time as seemed best to them, but He disciplines us for our good, so that we may share His holiness. All discipline for the moment seems not to be joyful, but sorrowful; yet to those who have been trained by it, afterwards it yields the peaceful fruit of righteousness.
>
> Hebrews 12:5–11

This is powerful! Here, the Hebrews writer contrasts sons and bastards (illegitimate children) by pointing out that bastards (fatherless men) are those who refuse discipline, while sons embrace correction, knowing that it breeds nobility in their lives. He goes on in the next chapter to further address all believers about leadership and submission. Read it for yourself:

> Obey your leaders and submit to them, for they keep watch over your souls as those who will give an account. Let them do this with joy and not with grief, for this would be unprofitable for you.
>
> Hebrews 13:17

If you grew up anything like me, you just want to turn the page on this book or maybe even throw the dang thing at the wall while yelling "*control freak!*" I really do get it. When I started following Jesus, I honestly didn't trust *anyone*, and I wasn't interested in learning how to change. I had been betrayed, abused and manipulated most of my childhood. When your father, who is supposed to teach you about love, is your abuser, you learn never to take your armor off (metaphorically speaking). . . . I mean, you sleep with it on. In fact, my stepfather used to wake me up by throwing a bucket of cold water on my head, so there was no safe place in my house!

The challenge is, the armor that protects you from hurt also isolates you from love. Furthermore, you can only be loved to the level that you can be hurt. So when you make an inner vow never to be hurt again, you have just moved into the ice castle of loveless isolation and frigid disconnection. Soon, you are starving for love and desperate to belong. Desperate, disconnected people look for love in all the wrong places to try to fill the huge hole in their soul, which leads to depression, low self-esteem and distress.

On the other hand, when you become courageous enough to take off your armor and learn how to trust, you ditch the orphan spirit, leave the land of bastardhood and begin the noble and amazing journey to true sonship.

> **When you become courageous enough to take off your armor and learn how to trust, you ditch the orphan spirit, leave the land of bastardhood and begin the noble and amazing journey to true sonship.**

Look at Hebrews 13:17 again. Did you notice that God has assigned leaders to "watch over your soul," and that they have to "give an account" to God for your well-being? This is so powerful! God has appointed a shepherd (one or more) to you, like a spiritual life coach, to help you succeed in your relationship with Him and accomplish your divine assignment.

EPIC
TAKEAWAYS

- The life-changing Voice: *My name is Jesus Christ, and you have what you requested! . . . My name is Jesus Christ, and you said if I healed your mother, you would serve Me. I am waiting!*

- The "Jesus People" meeting: A leader sat on the floor with Kathy and me and explained salvation in very simple terms. He taught us that we were now "born again," and that we were like spiritual children who needed a father. And then he found us one!

- The orphanage of isolation: If our fathers were disconnected, abusive or nonexistent, leaving us to fend for ourselves, then we don't trust authority figures because they didn't use their position to protect, provide for and promote us.

- Interdependent, not independent: God designed us to be bonded with others. Men need other men to connect to, and women need other women.

- Fathers in the faith: Teachers or tutors give us necessary instruction, but fathers are role models we should imitate. In other words, instructors teach what they know, but fathers impart who they are!

- Caring enough to confront: Men need fathers and leaders who love them enough to confront them, and who are wise enough to know when the time is right. In fact, all believers (men and women) need encouragement, love and instruction, but they also need discipline.

- Principles of love: You can only be loved to the level that you can be hurt. So when you make an inner vow never to be hurt again, you have just moved into the ice castle of loveless isolation and frigid disconnection. Soon, you are starving for love.

- Principles of sonship: On the other hand, when you become courageous enough to take off your armor and learn how to trust, you ditch the orphan spirit, leave the land of bastardhood and begin the noble and amazing journey to true sonship.

TWELVE

Finding Fathers

IF YOU'VE HAD THE GUTS to stay with me this long, you are probably asking questions like these: *How do I bond in a healthy way with leaders? How do I actually become a person who has a healthy spiritual leader/ father, or even a big brother, in my life? How do I find someone to disciple me, and/or find someone I can disciple?*

These are great questions, and for most people the answers are more practical than spiritual, at least at first. Most people tend to connect through common interests. For men, these interests might be cars, sports, family, church, work, etc. . . . someplace where guys talk and get to know each other. These conversations can be lighthearted, interesting and fun, but mostly they are superficial.

Yet to be discipled by someone, you must have a deep, bonded connection to that person. Therefore, the goal is to move from a casual relationship to something deeper—ultimately to be known and connected, and to belong with someone.

Forces of Disconnection

There are, however, invisible enemies warring against our soul and working to keep us isolated and alone. The greatest of these enemies is shame. Shame is the archenemy of strong connections and bonded relationships . . . the Goliath in our Promised Land and the devil against true discipleship. Shame is the fear that we are not smart enough, strong enough, pretty enough or handsome enough, spiritual enough, etc., to be loved and accepted. Shame says, *If you really knew me, you wouldn't like me because I am unqualified to be loved!*

Well-known clinical social worker and public speaker Brené Brown teaches that vulnerability breaks the power of shame that separates us from one another. She says, "Vulnerability is the birthplace of love, belonging, joy, courage, empathy, and creativity."[1] She goes on to define *vulnerability* as the ability to be *seen* and *known*. Yet we live in such a Photoshopped world, a place where many people hide behind pretend smiles, perfect family photos and social media pages littered with snapshots and videos of their best moments.

I love gathering with groups of men, but nowhere is this Photoshop dynamic more at play than when we feel the pressure to impress one another. I call it the "tree-peeing competition," and I hate it. You know what I mean. Men, like dogs, marking their territory, bragging about their greatest exploits, one-upping each other, name dropping, muscle flexing, who's the greatest . . . that's bull! I refuse to participate in these conversations because they are designed to make yourself look good by making others feel small, less than and inferior.

Shame spreads like wildfire in these situations because these interactions separate the hearts of men with walls of pride and gates of arrogance. The truth is that lurking just below the surface of all this chest-bumping, men-grunting, *Game of Thrones* behavior is usually a ton of insecurity, feelings of inferiority, the fear of inadequacy and tons and tons of shame. It's impossible to find real connection in a culture of rivalry.

Conversely, I have watched men put down their weapons and take off their armor during these gatherings. It happens when someone courageously steps up to the plate and shares his weakness, struggle and/or problems. There's something about "real and vulnerable" that unmasks pretenders and disarms phonies.

I watched this powerful dynamic take place in a meeting with about forty school of ministry leaders a few weeks ago. They are some of the greatest leaders in our movement. The team members were sharing stories of their amazing exploits, when suddenly, Steve (one of our best leaders) decided to break the perceived protocol and tell the team about his struggle. With tears streaming down his face, he stood up and proclaimed, "I've been in a war with insecurity and shame. Every time I get in the same room with you guys, I feel so small, and I'm afraid you guys are going to discover that I don't have what it takes to be in the same room with all of you great leaders!"

Before he could finish, another leader stood to her feet (this time a woman) and confessed the same struggle. Within minutes, half our leaders were on their feet, sharing their battle with shame.

> There's something about "real and vulnerable" that unmasks pretenders and disarms phonies.

For nearly two hours, leaders boldly shared their battle with feelings of inadequacy. There wasn't a dry eye in the room as leader after leader wept through his or her confession, ultimately capturing all our hearts in the vortex of their vulnerability.

That day, I felt as though God Himself had declared war against the shame that had imprisoned our very best leaders. Their honesty and vulnerability became powerful weapons of warfare that were blowing up the walls of the evil fortresses that separated them from each other. It has been weeks since that meeting occurred, yet the connection that took place that day still lingers. Now every gathering with this team feels like the special connection of a healthy family, a community of honest people loving on one another, building each other up and checking on each other's condition. The funny thing is, rumors of this team's vulnerability spread quickly to our other eight hundred staff members, which is creating the momentum for them also to take off their costumes and remove their masks. Our entire culture is beginning to vibrate with life and connection!

The apostle Paul struggled with weakness himself, yet he found so much meaning in it. In fact, the Lord gave him a thorn in the flesh that troubled him much of his life. In desperation, Paul prayed that God would deliver him from this affliction. The Lord's response to him floored me:

> And He has said to me, "My grace is sufficient for you, for power is perfected in weakness." Most gladly, therefore, I will rather boast about my

weaknesses, so that the power of Christ may dwell in me. Therefore I am well content with weaknesses, with insults, with distresses, with persecutions, with difficulties, for Christ's sake; for when I am weak, then I am strong.

2 Corinthians 12:9–10

This is a painful but powerful revelation! God purposely designed weakness into our lives. In fact, it's only in our weakness that His power is on full display. Paul went on to say that he liked to brag about his weakness, the places in his life where he sucked, his intense inadequacies, his tough situations, his persistent failures. If this is true of the great apostle Paul, then why should we hide behind the fig leaves of plastic personas, fallacies and fakes that disarm the power of Christ within us? I mean, if God purposely flawed us to empower His divine nature through us, why should we hide in shame or live with insecurity?

My Weakness

This reminds me of a situation that took place in my life about ten years ago. A chancellor of a Christian university in the United States offered me the opportunity to earn a doctorate from their university. I have no formal education beyond high school, so I was very interested in his offer and very excited about it. The plan was for me to write a doctoral dissertation on a subject and graduate with the current class.

To make matters even better, the university agreed to use my *Fashioned to Reign* book manuscript, which I had just completed, as my dissertation. All I had to do was reformat it. Several months passed, and things progressed quite quickly with the help of my personal assistant, Beth, who reformatted my entire manuscript to meet the requirements of my thesis.

Then one night I woke up out of a dead sleep, and I heard the Lord talking to me. He said, *You never asked Me if you could get a Ph.D. What do you think you're doing?*

Lord, I am kind of excited about getting my degree, I responded. *You know I have no education to speak of, so this will give me a lot of credibility with people. So, can I get a Ph.D.?* I questioned.

162

His answer was NO. He said, *Kris, if you have letters after your name, people will think you can do all of this, and we both know that you can't! You were born to be an example of what I can do with weakness. When people observe your life and see who you have become, and what you have accomplished in the midst of your faults, failures, flaws and frailties, they will know that your greatness is rooted in Me. Your life was meant to be an inspiration for the weak and the broken. Many people will put their trust in Me because of what I do through you. Now, call the university and cancel your doctorate!*

"When people observe your life and see who you have become, and what you have accomplished in the midst of your faults, failures, flaws and frailties, they will know that your greatness is rooted in Me."

I was bummed, but I obeyed!

Authenticity

Authenticity is another one of those character qualities that destroys shame and builds connection. Authenticity is the ability to let go of who you think you should be, so you can be who you really are. We all live with this crazy tension in the core of our being—we desperately want to fit in, while at the same time we deeply desire to stand out. A great divide takes place in our hearts when we become a copy of someone else in order to fit in and stand out. This feeds *impostor syndrome*, which is the feeling that you are inadequate or inferior, and you therefore become terrified of being unmasked, found out and/or discovered.

The truth is, if you've become a cheap imitation of someone else instead of an original masterpiece of God's imagination, then you have to work every day to feed the monster of illusion as you masquerade in the costume of copycat confusion. It's exhausting! Of course, this dynamic isolates you from true discipleship because discipleship requires you to bond at the place of vulnerability. Think about it: It's impossible to be honestly vulnerable when you are being dishonestly identified. Personally, I've come to the place in my life at which I would rather be hated for who I am than be loved for who I am not!

Many of us fall into the spirit of comparison, measuring our value and success by comparing ourselves to others. This is a cheap trick of the devil that leads us to discouragement and further disconnection. Paul put it like this:

> For we are not bold to class or compare ourselves with some of those who commend themselves; but when they measure themselves by themselves and compare themselves with themselves, they are without understanding.
>
> 2 Corinthians 10:12

Comparison is the kryptonite of the twenty-first century, with many people determining their self-worth by the size of their social pages or the reach of their posts. You must find your sense of purpose and self-worth in the Lord by becoming intensely aware of His thoughts toward you and His love for you. When you accept *who* you are in *Him*, and thus fall in love with the person you see in the mirror of authenticity, then you become a welcome mat for deep personal relationships.

> When you accept who you are in the Lord, and thus fall in love with the person you see in the mirror of authenticity, then you become a welcome mat for deep personal relationships.

In fact, being "comfortable in your own skin" is the primary catalyst for covenant connections and radical discipleship. If someone doesn't like and enjoy the real you, then why would you want that person to mentor you? If you become authentic, I guarantee you that not everyone will like you. But if those same people would like you for who you pretend to be, then in reality they still don't like you, but they just don't know it yet! So I double-dog dare you to learn to love yourself and let the best "real you" be on full display every day.

Humility

Humility is probably the most important quality of discipleship, yet it also is the most misdefined. So let me begin this conversation by saying that humility is not feeling bad about yourself, demeaning yourself or embracing low self-esteem. In simple terms, humility means that you are teachable, correctable, pliable, leadable, and that you are a servant. True humility is the one quality that, almost all by itself, can lead to real success in life and love.

The apostle Peter put it like this: "Therefore humble yourselves under the mighty hand of God, that He may exalt you at the proper time (1 Peter 5:6). On the other hand, Solomon wrote, "Pride goes before destruction, a haughty spirit before a fall" (Proverbs 16:18 NIV). Let me put it in simple terms so it's easy to comprehend:

$$Humility + Nothing = Promotion$$
$$Pride \ \& \ Arrogance + Nothing = Humiliation$$

This truth is at work in us no matter who we are, how long we pray, how many good things we have done or who likes us. In fact, we may be right about a matter and another person may be wrong, but *Right + Arrogance* still *= Humiliation*. This dynamic becomes crystal clear when we consider biblical history. God raised up leaders who repeatedly became full of themselves and fell. Think about kings like Uzziah, Hezekiah, Nebuchadnezzar and even Solomon himself. God exalted them, and then they became arrogant and fell.

Here, for example, is God's commentary on King Uzziah: "When he became strong, his heart was so proud that he acted corruptly, and he was unfaithful to the LORD his God" (2 Chronicles 26:16). On the other hand, God sent Elijah to prophesy against Ahab, one of the wickedest kings in Israel's history (the king who was married to Jezebel). But one time, Ahab humbled himself when he heard the prophetic word. Then God spoke to Elijah and said, "Do you see how Ahab has humbled himself before Me? Because he has humbled himself before Me, I will not bring the evil in his days" (1 Kings 21:29). Wow!

If arrogance and humility had such powerful negative and positive effects on the kings of old, think about how important attitudes are in our relationship with God and men today. True discipleship can only take place in the seedbed of humility, which must be proactively cultivated in the hearts of both those who are being discipled and those who are doing the discipling.

I have personally discipled many people over the last four decades, and I've concluded that humility is *the key factor* in seeing people I am pouring my life into change. The challenge is that many times when people ask for advice, what they really want is encouragement, or a stamp of approval on their self-will, or agreement with their idea. Let me be clear that encouragement is paramount in the life of all believers, but so is direction, correction and discipline.

> **True discipleship can only take place in the seedbed of humility, which must be proactively cultivated in the hearts of both those who are being discipled and those who are doing the discipling.**

As I pointed out earlier, discipleship requires us to be teachable, correctable and influenceable. If you are longing for someone to disciple you, but you are not ready to change, or if you are not really ready to listen to a leader who is more mature in the Lord than you, then your heart posture is not ready to be discipled.

The apostle James put it like this: "In humility receive the word implanted, which is able to save your souls" (James 1:21). James connects humility with receptivity and reminds us that the Word can't just be heard; it must be implanted to produce its lifesaving power within us. The Greek word *save* in this passage is *sozo*, and it means cured, recovered, restored, healed, delivered and saved.[2] True discipleship is not controlling; it is empowering, life-giving and destiny fulfilling. It is the catalyst for salvation on every level of our triune being—spirit, soul and body.

EPIC
TAKEAWAYS

- Deep discipleship: To be discipled by someone, you must have a deep, bonded connection to that person. Therefore, the goal is to move from a casual relationship to something deeper—ultimately to be known and connected, and to belong with someone.

- The shameful disconnect: Shame is the forceful disconnector, the archenemy of strong connections and bonded relationships. Shame says, *If you really knew me, you wouldn't like me because I am unqualified to be loved!*

- The shame breaker: Vulnerability breaks the power of shame that separates us from one another. It's the ability to be *seen* and *known*, and it's also the birthplace of joy, happiness, creativity, belonging and love.

- The unmasking: There's just something about "real and vulnerable" that unmasks pretenders and disarms phonies. This unmasking happens when someone courageously steps up to the plate and shares his or her weakness, struggle and/or problems.

- Powerful demolition: Honesty and vulnerability act as powerful weapons of warfare that blow up and demolish the walls of the evil fortresses that can separate us from each other.

- Weakness on display: Only in our weakness is God's power is on full display. Why should we hide behind shame or insecurity when God empowers His divine nature through us and our weakness?

- The *impostor syndrome*: Copycats suffer from this. It's the feeling that you are inadequate or inferior; therefore, you become terrified of being unmasked, found out and/or discovered. Be authentically yourself instead!

- The devil's cheap trick: The spirit of comparison is a cheap trick of the devil that leads us into measuring our value and success by comparing ourselves to others. This only leads to discouragement and further disconnection.

- Finding your true self: You must find your sense of purpose and self-worth in the Lord by becoming intensely aware of His thoughts toward you and His love for you. Accept *who* you are in *Him* and fall in love with the person you see in the mirror of authenticity. Let the best "real you" be on display every day!

- Positive change's *key factor*: Humility is *the key factor* in change. True discipleship can only take place in the seedbed of humility, when we are willing to listen and be teachable, correctable and influenceable.

THIRTEEN

Spiritual Men

TRUE FATHERS ARE MORE THAN BREADWINNERS who "bring home the bacon." They must also "bring home the Bread of Life." As I stated earlier, fathers promote, protect and provide for their families. Yet the tridimensional role and responsibility of fatherhood is *first* spiritual, and then natural.

I can hear the comments now: *I don't want to be so heavenly minded that I'm no earthly good!*

I get that, but from an eternal perspective, if you aren't heavenly minded, you won't be any earthly good! What I am really trying to say is that humans are tridimensional creatures—spirit, soul and body. The nature of fatherhood is for a father to provide for, promote and protect every aspect of his family. For example, fathers are commissioned to be courageous. They don't have the luxury of retreating in the face of danger. Fathers are called to run toward the sound of trouble and engage any hostility that is perpetuated against their families. They are the first into danger! They send a loud message to all hostiles that there will be resistance to hurting this family . . . there will be a noble defender ready to protect this lineage.

Yet there are lots of men who seem to protect their families well physically, but spiritually speaking, "Amber Alerts" are going off in their homes because the devil has abducted one or more of their children. These fathers are not in tune enough to the spirit realm even to know their kids are missing!

It's important to understand that the greatest threat to our family's well-being often lies in the invisible realm. Therefore, protecting our family isn't just a Rambo-like act of courage in which we run into a burning building to rescue our children from some depraved kidnapper. Instead, we have to take our place on the spiritual walls of the family castle and watch in prayer for hostiles who would try to deceive our kids into unlocking the castle gate and letting them in.

Here is a great word picture of what I am trying to explain. This was spoken by the prophet Isaiah about five hundred years before Christ:

On your walls, O Jerusalem, I have appointed watchmen; all day and all night they will never keep silent. You who remind the LORD, take no rest for yourselves; and give Him no rest until He establishes and makes Jerusalem a praise in the earth.

Isaiah 62:6–7

Crisis Christianity

It's incumbent upon us to take practical responsibility for our own spiritual life and thus grow our "inner man" proactively (whether we are a man or a woman). If we only seek God when we are in a crisis, then He is kind enough to allow our lives to be a series of crises, which are usually strung together by short intervals of peace. These "peace breaks" give us the opportunity to seek the Lord out of love instead of out of pain, and thus change the ecosystem of our relationship with Jesus—ultimately delivering us from "crisis Christianity."

Speaking of crisis Christianity, I was at a men's conference a few years back where the apostle Guillermo Maldonado was challenging the men to be godly with a strong exhortation. He said, "Some men go to the gym every day to work out their body, but they don't take ten minutes to pray. They have a $100,000 body and a ten-cent spirit!" He continued his righteous rant, "Some men know all the stats of their sports teams, their names and their history, but they can't name five characters in the Bible. Some spend more time with their fantasy sports team than they do with their reality God!"

Yikes! I must admit that his word was a little hard to hear, but it was incredibly convicting. Guillermo finished with this profound statement: "We don't have moral authority to rebuke the evil we practice ourselves!"[1] It would be like giving an offering at church to end sex trafficking, while you are addicted to porn at home.

> If we only seek God when we are in a crisis, then He is kind enough to allow our lives to be a series of crises.

Now, let me be clear: We don't have to be spiritual giants, but it is incumbent upon us to be spiritual men. As you read this exhortation, you might be feeling shame or inadequacy. But our own deep sense of spiritual inadequacy will not be defeated by retreating; it will only be dethroned as we press into God and learn how to destroy the works of the devil. We simply can't conquer what we refuse to confront! Furthermore, our personal victories become our family's corporate covering. Therefore, every foe we defeat in our own life is one less foe our family will have to face in theirs.

Becoming a Spiritual Man

What does it mean to be a "spiritual man"? (Or to be a spiritual woman, since this question can apply to us all.) It begins with asking Jesus into your heart and dedicating the rest of your life to following Him. Jesus said that this simple act of giving up your will and taking on the will of your heavenly Father enacts a spiritual birth that is described as becoming "born again."

The next step is called "repentance," and it begins by confessing any sin that the Holy Spirit brings to your mind when you are talking to Him, including the sin of unforgiveness.

Once you have "confessed your sins," it's important that you forgive the people in your life who have hurt, betrayed and/or disappointed you. It may even be necessary to go back to some people and "clean up your mess" with them. This is called "bringing forth fruit of repentance."

> It's essential to understand the massive ramifications of baptism. This simple act of obedience unleashes the power of heaven on you.

This process of submitting your will to your heavenly Father's will, connecting with the Holy Spirit for advice, confessing your sins and cleaning up your messes isn't a onetime event. It is the ecosystem of life in the Spirit, the way in which you will manage your life in God.

It's also important for you to be "baptized" in water as an act of obedience in following Jesus. He Himself put it this way: "Go into all the world and preach the gospel to all creation. He who has believed and has been baptized shall be saved; but he who has disbelieved shall be condemned" (Mark 16:15–16). It's essential to understand the massive ramifications of baptism. This simple act of obedience unleashes the power of heaven on you. The brilliant-minded apostle Paul put it like this:

> Do you not know that all of us who have been baptized into Christ Jesus have been baptized into His death? Therefore we have been buried with Him through baptism into death, so that as Christ was raised from the dead through the glory of the Father, so we too might walk in newness of life. For if we have become united with Him in the likeness of His death, certainly we shall also be in the likeness of His resurrection, knowing this, that our old self was crucified with Him, in order that our body of sin might be done away with, so that we would no longer be slaves to sin; for he who has died is freed from sin.
>
> Now if we have died with Christ, we believe that we shall also live with Him, knowing that Christ, having been raised from the dead, is never to die again; death no longer is master over Him. For the death that He died, He died to sin once for all; but the life that He lives, He lives to God. Even so consider yourselves to be dead to sin, but alive to God in Christ Jesus.
>
> Romans 6:3–11

This passage is deep, and it might make you feel a bit overwhelmed, so let me unpack it. There are two kinds of "acts" the Bible instructs us to perform: *acts of remembrance* and *prophetic acts*. We carry out acts of remembrance as a way to remember the powerful works God has done for us. The best New Testament example of this kind of act is Communion. Here is a passage that makes my point:

> I received from the Lord that which I also delivered to you, that the Lord Jesus in the night in which He was betrayed took bread; and when He had given thanks, He broke it and said, "This is My body, which is for you; do this in *remembrance* of Me." In the same way He took the cup also after supper, saying, "This cup is the new covenant in My blood; do this, as often as you drink it, in *remembrance* of Me." For as often as you eat this bread and drink the cup, you proclaim the Lord's death until He comes.
>
> 1 Corinthians 11:23–26, emphasis added

Acts of remembrance are important because they remind us that nothing is impossible with God. If He did something before, He can and will do it again!

The Power of Prophetic Acts

The second kind of act we are invited to participate in is a *prophetic act*, which I briefly mentioned earlier in the book. This is not an act of remembrance, but an act of *supernatural power*. What I am saying is that the physical obedience of a prophetic act brings about a powerful spiritual release. Let me illustrate this principle by recounting a wild story from the Bible. There was a guy named Naaman who was the captain of the Aramean army. The guy was a famous valiant warrior, but he was also a leper. Leprosy was thought to be contagious, so it was kind of hard to make friends and influence people when you had to walk down the street and yell, "*Unclean! Unclean!*" (That's the understatement of the century.)

The story goes that the Aramean army fought against the Israelites and consequently captured some prisoners of war, including a young Jewish girl. By some divine intervention, the girl became the servant of Naaman's wife. One day, this servant girl had a conversation with his wife and told her stories about an Israeli prophet named Elisha, who was famous for performing supernatural acts, including healing leprosy.

You can read the whole story in 2 Kings 5, but the short version is that through a series of circumstances, Naaman finally ended up traveling to Samaria to seek help from Elisha the prophet. When Naaman arrived at Elisha's house, Elisha refused to come out. Instead, the prophet sent his servant, Gehazi, out to represent him. The servant instructed Naaman to dip seven times in the Jordan River, after which he would be clean of leprosy.

Naaman was infuriated by the lack of spiritual drama and the ridiculously simple solution Elisha proposed through his servant. He rode off in a huff with his army in tow, telling his soldiers that he wouldn't submit to such a ludicrous demand. But his servants convinced him to take a risk and dip in the Jordan anyway, basically telling him, "What do you have to lose?" When Naaman came up out of the water the seventh time, his skin was picture-perfect and his leprosy was gone!

> **Baptism is a prophetic act that unleashes the power of heaven in our souls, killing the old sinful man and resurrecting the new, righteous man from the cords of death.**

By now you are probably wondering, *What does Naaman the leper's story have to do with me?*

Good question! I am exposing you to the power of a prophetic act. Like Naaman, we were all born with this hereditary disease called sin. Sin is a heart disease that destroys us from the inside out, devastates our relationships and separates us from our Creator. Baptism, however, is a prophetic act that unleashes the power of heaven in our souls, killing the old sinful man and resurrecting the new, righteous man from the cords of death.

Think of it like this: First you are dunked under the water; this is the part of the prophetic act that reenacts our burial *with* Christ. We literally died (past tense) with Christ on the cross, and we were entombed with Him in the grave. Look at Romans 6:3–4 again: "Do you not know that all of us who have been baptized into Christ Jesus have been baptized into His death? Therefore we have been buried with Him through baptism into death."

But the next part of this prophetic act is the most powerful. We rise out of the water as Jesus rose from the tomb, as a new creation. The Greek word for *new* here means *prototype*, as in "never before created." We no longer have a sin nature, because our old, leprous man died and our new man has the righteous nature of Jesus!

Okay, check out the second part of Romans 6:4 again: "As Christ was raised from the dead through the glory of the Father, so we too might walk in newness of life." And in verse 11, here is the triumphant climax of baptism: "Even so consider yourselves to be dead to sin, but alive to God in Christ Jesus."

Can you imagine how this prophetic act can change your life? Like Naaman, we were living in the leprosy of shame, knowing that evil was lurking within, but having no answer . . . no solution . . . no way to kill the monster in the cellar of our souls. We spent our days trying to hold the cellar door closed, desperately hoping that the monster wouldn't someday gain enough strength to rip the door off its hinges and destroy everything and everyone we love. But suddenly, something powerful took place—we stepped into the water of baptism and drowned that sucker! For the first time in our lives, the chilling screams from the basement floor of our very souls are silent, and the pounding on the cellar door has ceased. Our fear of harboring a monster, and our shame at being a righteous poser, have disintegrated in the light of our new nature and the power of the resurrection.

How Then Shall We Live?

The truth is, so many of us are trying to do with discipline what can only be accomplished through resurrection power. It's not that discipline isn't important. It is. In the same way that a proper diet and exercise increase our physical strength and health, spiritual disciplines cause our spiritual

> We can't discipline ourselves into a new nature. We need the power of God to deliver us from the monster of our old nature.

man to grow in strength and health. But we can't discipline ourselves into a new nature. We need the power of God to deliver us from the monster of our old nature. Then we can break our old habits and unhealthy ways of thinking, because they were rooted in a nature that is now dead. They literally have no roots left in our soul.

The apostle Paul goes on in Romans 6:12–14 to teach us how to live as new creatures in Jesus. He writes,

Therefore do not let sin reign in your mortal body so that you obey its lusts, and do not go on presenting the members of your body to sin as instruments of unrighteousness; but present yourselves to God as those alive from the dead, and your members as instruments of righteousness to God. For sin shall not be master over you, for you are not under law but under grace.

Now we can change our habits because we have a new nature. We are no longer sinners, but saints . . . we are sons and daughters of our heavenly Father . . . and heirs to the throne!

Spiritual Inheritance

As we fathers find our footing in the foundations of Jesus and begin to develop a rhythm in the Spirit through connection with the Lord, a powerful secondary impact takes place in our homes and among our families. A spiritual ecosystem is established. Let me express it like this: Whenever our children catch us having a private conversation with God in prayer, they capture a glimpse into the power of the age to come that's being infused into the family trust.

Furthermore, as our kids view our prayers answered, battles won, necessities provided, relationships restored, people healed, souls delivered and so much more, they have a front-row seat in the academy of future victories for themselves.

In other words, not only are we taking ground in the Spirit for our families, causing them to enjoy the benefits of our friendship with the Father, and paving the way for them to live a productive spiritual life through inheriting our victories, but we are also modeling a spiritual life in God. We are demonstrating for them, through our own spiritual connection and disciplines, what it means to be a disciple.

EPIC
TAKEAWAYS

- *First* spiritual, then natural: True fathers are more than breadwinners who "bring home the bacon." They must also "bring home the Bread of Life."
- Watchmen on the walls: The greatest threat to our family's well-being often lies in the invisible realm. We fathers have to take our place on the spiritual walls of the family castle and watch in prayer for hostiles.
- Crisis Christianity: When we seek the Lord out of love instead of out of pain (crises), it changes the ecosystem of our relationship with Jesus—ultimately delivering us from "crisis Christianity."
- Father, Your will be done: The simple act of giving up your will and taking on the will of your heavenly Father enacts a spiritual birth that is described as becoming "born again."
- The next steps: After being born again comes repentance, confession of sin, cleaning up messes, bringing forth fruit of repentance and being baptized.
- Massive ramifications: The simple act of obedience in being baptized unleashes the power of heaven in our souls, killing the old, sinful man and resurrecting the new, righteous man from the cords of death.
- New creation prototypes: After baptism in water, we no longer have a sin nature, because our old, leprous man died and our new man has the righteous nature of Jesus!
- Discipline *and* deliverance: Discipline is important, but we can't discipline ourselves into a new nature. We need the power of God to deliver us from the monster of our old nature. Then we can change our habits because we have a new nature.
- A spiritual ecosystem: As our kids view our prayers answered, battles won, necessities provided, relationships restored, people healed, souls delivered and so much more, they have a front-row seat in the academy of future victories for themselves.

FOURTEEN

Dismantling Genderless Discipleship

ONE OF THE GREATEST CHALLENGES of the twenty-first-century Church is finding men who know how to father and/or disciple others. There are so many leaders who are more like the elder brother in the prodigal son story than like the father who is happy to have his wayward son back and is ready to restore him. I call this the *elder brother syndrome*. It's the dynamic in which the elder brothers are competing with the people they are supposed to be leading. When we are competing with the people we lead, we create a controlling environment instead of an empowering environment. This doesn't bring out the best in the people we are mentoring.

Let me be clear—discipline is an important part of discipleship (as I pointed out in the previous chapters), but discipline is not punishing, shaming or reducing people with our words, actions or attitudes. Instead, godly discipline is rooted in the fact that I love you too much to leave you the way you are. I am therefore compelled to communicate with you how your life is negatively affecting your destiny and/or the well-being of others.

Discipleship must be rooted in faith for the people we are mentoring. In other words, we must believe in the people we lead and have a deep sense of God's divine purpose for them. Personally, I got saved when I believed in Jesus, but I began to be transformed the day I realized that He believed in me!

For most of my Christian journey, I've heard people say things like, "We need to hold people accountable for their life." I think accountability is important, if we define the word accurately. *Accountability* means giving an account for your ability, not your disability! I love the way my friend Paul Manwaring, puts it: "Accountability isn't making sure someone doesn't smoke, but helping to make sure they are on fire." The purpose of discipleship isn't to give your spiritual sons or daughters a character MRI every time you meet. Discipleship is not faultfinding! The goal of healthy discipleship is to help people fulfill their God-given purpose by first discovering their divine identity, purpose and calling, and then assisting them in developing their character, gifts and skills so you can help deploy them into their divine destiny.

> **Personally, I got saved when I believed in Jesus, but I began to be transformed the day I realized that He believed in me!**

Masculine Mentorship

Let's look at a page taken from a private letter the apostle Paul wrote to his spiritual son Timothy and see what we can learn about spiritual sonship and fatherhood. Paul wrote,

> Discipline yourself for the purpose of godliness; for bodily discipline is only of little profit, but godliness is profitable for all things, since it holds promise for the present life and also for the life to come. It is a trustworthy statement deserving full acceptance. For it is for this we labor and strive, because we have fixed our hope on the living God, who is the Savior of all men, especially of believers.
>
> Prescribe and teach these things. Let no one look down on your youthfulness, but rather in speech, conduct, love, faith and purity, show yourself an example of those who believe. Until I come, give attention to the public reading of Scripture, to exhortation and teaching. Do not neglect the spiritual

gift within you, which was bestowed on you through prophetic utterance with the laying on of hands by the presbytery. Take pains with these things; be absorbed in them, so that your progress will be evident to all. Pay close attention to yourself and to your teaching; persevere in these things, for as you do this you will ensure salvation both for yourself and for those who hear you.

1 Timothy 4:7–16

Paul exhorted Tim to embrace the kind of godly disciplines that have eternal significance. He goes on to describe those disciplines specifically as exhortation, teaching and the special, spiritual gift that was imparted to Timothy when the presbytery laid their hands on him. He was requiring Timothy to be accountable for his God-given abilities (account-ability), while also encouraging him to embrace righteous character.

I love how Paul told Timothy not to let anyone look down on him because he was young, but rather . . . and then he gave him a list of things that would cause Tim's congregation to look up to him. In other words, Paul didn't tell Timothy to confront the people who were looking down on him. Instead, he instructed him to man up: "Work harder on your gifts, get better at preaching and teaching, persevere, take pains with your progress. . . . Come on, Timothy, you can do this!" It was a kind kick in the butt by a man who deeply loved and believed in him.

Paul and Timothy's relationship is a great discipleship model for us as twenty-first-century men who need a fathering, masculine model of mentorship to follow. Men need encouragement and understanding, but we must leave our mothers' aprons and the weenie, low-expectation, crybaby mentoring that is often depicted in much of the Church. People need to be challenged, exhorted and even prodded at times to fight through their fears, get off the couch of comfort and engage in the battle to advance the Kingdom in them and around them.

> **People need to be challenged, exhorted and even prodded at times to fight through their fears, get off the couch of comfort and engage in the battle to advance the Kingdom in them and around them.**

183

Paul's love for Timothy is so evident through all his letters, but he refused to let Tim be a wimp. Check out this piece of Paul's second letter to this spiritual son:

> I call to remembrance the genuine faith that is in you, which dwelt first in your grandmother Lois and your mother Eunice, and I am persuaded is in you also. Therefore I remind you to stir up the gift of God which is in you through the laying on of my hands. For God has not given us a spirit of fear, but of power and of love and of a sound mind.
>
> Therefore do not be ashamed of the testimony of our Lord, nor of me His prisoner, but share with me in the sufferings for the gospel according to the power of God.
>
> 2 Timothy 1:5–8 NKJV

Again, Paul encourages Timothy by recounting the Christian legacy passed down to him by his grandmother and mother. Yet Paul knows that with much authority comes much responsibility; therefore, he prods Timothy to "stir up the gift of God" (verse 6). This Greek phrase can also be interpreted as "Take your gift and put it in the fire!" This translation makes more sense to me in light of the exhortation that follows: "God has not given us a spirit of fear, but of power and of love and of a sound mind. . . . Share with me in the sufferings" (verses 7–8).

Bear with me as we look at one last excerpt from Paul's profound letter to his disciple, Timothy:

> You therefore, my son, be strong in the grace that is in Christ Jesus. The things which you have heard from me in the presence of many witnesses, entrust these to faithful men who will be able to teach others also. Suffer hardship with me, as a good soldier of Christ Jesus. No soldier in active service entangles himself in the affairs of everyday life, so that he may please the one who enlisted him as a soldier. Also if anyone competes as an athlete, he does not win the prize unless he competes according to the rules. The hard-working farmer ought to be the first to receive his share of the crops. Consider what I say, for the Lord will give you understanding in everything.
>
> 2 Timothy 2:1–7

I hope you are capturing the intense theme that is at the core of Paul and Timothy's relationship. It's depicted by phrases like *hard work*, *suffer hardship*, *intense warfare*, *be strong*, *don't be afraid*. In other words, don't be a wimp, a whiner or a weenie. Put your big-boy pants on and get after your calling!

Discipling men isn't a game of Old Maid or hopscotch; it's a lot more like digging trenches in the heat of the day, with a handpick, in the hard soil of men's hearts, to plant the seeds of righteousness for a harvest of souls. Mentoring men is not for the faint of heart. It takes guts! And yes, it's true that we live in different conditions today than Paul and Timothy experienced in the first-century Church. For instance, we Americans are not (yet) being martyred for our faith. Yet the challenge of fathering men who are slugging their way out of the cesspool of immorality, covered in the dark slime of pornography, while dragging the ball and chain of abandonment, rejection and hatred, is no picnic!

Furthermore, the global Church has been so affected by the lack of fathering and the influx of the feminist spirit that men are literally leaving the Church in droves. Men aren't women. I am so glad the Church is embracing women and empowering them to lead alongside men! As a matter of fact, I wrote a book about this powerful dynamic titled *Fashioned to Reign*, as I mentioned before. Yet we must understand that the cultural battle raging in the world to emasculate men and homogenize the genders is

> The cultural battle raging in the world to emasculate men and homogenize the genders is destroying the beauty and strengths of the diversity of the genders. One of the fruits of this is genderless discipleship.

destroying the beauty and strengths of the diversity of the genders. One of the fruits of this is genderless discipleship, meaning that we shepherd men as if they are women and refuse to differentiate between the sexes. We cannot disciple men and women in the same way and have the same powerful outcomes, because each gender requires specific types of leadership to be fully actualized.

I'm not saying that every aspect of discipleship should be different between men and women. I'm simply pointing out that men need masculine leadership to develop their manly qualities that facilitate their unique, God-given purpose and calling.

Leading Men Like Men

I have so many stories that personify the dynamic of leading men in a way that challenges them to embrace their high call in God. For example, I was discipling about ten young men who were in high school in the early eighties. These were rugged mountain men who were born in the mountains of the Trinity Alps. I decided to start a 6:00 a.m. prayer meeting before school with them, to teach them how to sacrifice for Jesus and how to be spiritually minded. The only problem was, I couldn't get any of them to come to the prayer meeting. I finally told them that they couldn't come to any prayer meetings unless they were personally invited by me. Then I invited just one young man named Tom to the next prayer meeting. I instructed him not to tell anyone that he was invited, and not to invite anyone else.

Tom came to the next prayer meeting, but he was late, so I locked the door of the church and told him from inside the door that if he wanted to be part of this prayer meeting, he had to come on time. "No one who's late is allowed to come to pray with me," I insisted.

Tom was ten minutes early for the next prayer meeting. Over the next three months, we prayed together a couple of times a week. Our prayer times were amazing! Then one morning, Tom asked if he could invite Sam to the prayer meeting. I quizzed him intently about the level of Sam's spirituality and told him I would pray about Sam's participation. A month later, I invited Sam to join us. I said nothing to Sam about being on time or the importance of consistency, but I'm sure Tom informed him about our standard, because Sam was always there on time. The three of us prayed together for months, and soon the word was out that there was an exclusive group of men who loved God enough to get up early and seek Him.

As time passed, Tom and Sam asked if we could invite others from our youth group to our prayer meeting, and again I delayed my answer and then later let them join. It was so beautiful to see all these young people getting up early in the morning to love on God. But as time went on, the prayer team slipped into complacency and guys started coming late to prayer. Consequently, I locked the door again and sent them away to think about their commitment. Furthermore, if they missed a meeting without an important reason, I took them off the prayer team and let them know that this meeting was *only* for those who were serious about Jesus and who wanted to develop the spiritual gifts that I saw in them. The funny thing is, the guys always came back and asked for another chance, which of course I granted.

Ultimately, I had a couple dozen kids praying twice a week at 6:00 a.m. for years. Subsequently, our youth group flourished, both numerically and spiritually, and some of those kids are in full-time ministry today!

Harsh! you say.

Maybe, but men need a challenge that's worth dying for. The truth is, until you have something to die for, you never really live! Jesus was always challenging people to death and raising the bar of discipleship. Check out this exhortation:

> Then Jesus said to His disciples, "If anyone wishes to come after Me, he must deny himself, and take up his cross and follow Me. For whoever wishes to save his life will lose it; but whoever loses his life for My sake will find it."
>
> Matthew 16:24–25

But wait, Jesus takes it up another notch in John's gospel:

> Jesus said to them, "Truly, truly, I say to you, unless you eat the flesh of the Son of Man and drink His blood, you have no life in yourselves. He who eats My flesh and drinks My blood has eternal life, and I will raise him up on the last day."
>
> John 6:53–54

You might be wondering where I'm going with all of this. I'm simply pointing out that we need mentors—spiritual fathers who know how to lead in a way that challenges men and women to become disciples of Christ and give their lives for something much greater than themselves.

> **Great leaders catalyze the divine DNA that lies dormant in so many believers and is dying to be awakened—or more accurately, to be resurrected to life.**

Great leaders catalyze the divine DNA that lies dormant in so many believers and is dying to be awakened—or more accurately, to be resurrected to life. This is more powerful than finding a just cause to die for. This is about empowering people into their divine call and thus giving them something to *live* for!

Metaphorically speaking, we need leaders who will walk the earth proclaiming, "Lazarus, come forth!" Great fathers are those who call forth people out of the graves of small thinking, destructive lifestyles and dead-end roads of rhetoric, and thrust them into the *great* adventure of God's superior Kingdom.

EPIC
TAKEAWAYS

- The *elder brother syndrome*: This is the dynamic in which elder brothers compete with the people they're supposed to be leading. When we do that, we create a controlling environment instead of an empowering environment. This doesn't bring out the best in the people we are mentoring.
- Transformational discipleship: We must believe in the people we lead and have a deep sense of God's divine purpose for them. *Accountability* means having them give an account for their ability, not their disability!
- Masculine mentorship: Men need a fathering, masculine model of mentorship to follow. They need encouragement and understanding, but they must leave their mothers' aprons and the weenie, low-expectation, crybaby mentoring that is often depicted in much of the Church.
- Not for the faint of heart: The challenge of fathering men who are slugging their way out of the cesspool of immorality, covered in the dark slime of pornography, while dragging the ball and chain of abandonment, rejection and hatred, is no picnic!
- Men aren't women: Genderless discipleship means we shepherd men as if they are women and refuse to differentiate between the sexes. We can't do that and have the same powerful outcomes, because each gender requires specific types of leadership to be fully actualized.
- A challenge worth living for: The truth is, until you have something to die for, you never really live! Jesus was always challenging people to death and raising the bar of discipleship.
- The role of great fathers: Great fathers are those who call forth people out of the graves of small thinking, destructive lifestyles and dead-end roads of rhetoric, and thrust them into the *great* adventure of God's superior Kingdom.

FIFTEEN

Leaving a Legacy

THE STORY OF THE PRODIGAL SON ends beautifully in the Bible, but as I have outlined in the chapters of this book, the successful reentry and reconciliation of family members, especially fathers, has been rare in today's society. Many men leave their pregnant wives or girlfriends because they feel overwhelmed, unqualified or ill prepared. Of course, abandoning his child is against the fathering instincts that are latent in every man. Consequently, this breeds shame and guilt in the hearts of prodigal fathers. Shame and guilt further disqualify these men, causing them to further disconnect from the mother of their children. Disconnection and isolation lead to deeper feelings of condemnation, which result in further withdrawing. I think you get the idea. . . . This is the cycle in the twenty-first-century poverty that is destroying our families.

This dysfunctional ecosystem stands in stark contrast to one of the most powerful principles of Kingdom fathering, which is that *you can't become what you haven't seen or heard*. Much as a lion teaches its cubs to hunt, or as an eagle trains its offspring to fly, dads teach sons how to father their children. But what would happen if a lion cub were raised in a zoo or an eagle in a cage, and then some well-meaning person "gave it its freedom" and released it into the wild at four or five years old? We don't need to do a bunch of research to know the answer to that; it wouldn't survive. As I have been saying for years, it's hard to be ready for the jungle when you train in the zoo! It's tough for men to be ready to lead a family when they have been, metaphorically speaking, raised in an orphanage, institutionalized, hand-fed and "protected" by the bars of poverty.

To combat poverty, our often well-meaning governmental agencies give money to poor people without any relationship, agreed-upon outcomes, accountability and/or vision for a legacy, which ultimately funds fatherless poverty. Robert Rector, a member of the Heritage Foundation, talked about the side effects of government programs on fatherlessness and marriage. He wrote,

> The burgeoning welfare state has promoted single parenthood in two ways. First, means-tested welfare programs . . . financially enable single parenthood. It is difficult for single mothers with a high school degree or less to support children without the aid of another parent. Means-tested welfare programs substantially reduce this difficulty by providing extensive support to single parents. Welfare thereby reduces the financial need for marriage. Since the beginning of the War on Poverty, less educated mothers have increasingly become married to the welfare state and to the U.S. taxpayer rather than to the fathers of their children.
>
> . . . Welfare began to serve as a substitute for a husband in the home, and low-income marriage began to disappear. As husbands left the home, the need for more welfare to support single mothers increased. The War on Poverty created a destructive feedback loop: Welfare promoted the decline of marriage, which generated a need for more welfare.
>
> A second major problem is that the means-tested welfare system actively penalizes low-income parents who do marry. . . . If a low-income single mother marries an employed father, her welfare benefits will generally be substantially reduced. The mother can maximize welfare by remaining unmarried and keeping the father's income "off the books."
>
> . . . Overall, the federal government operates over 80 means-tested welfare programs that provide cash, food, housing, medical care, and social services to poor and low-income individuals. Each program contains marriage penalties similar to those described.[1]

The greatest victims of fatherlessness are children, as they did nothing to cause or deserve their situation. It's understandable that our welfare programs are designed to help fund their needs.

As a matter of fact, when my father died, our family lived on the government's welfare program for several years. I am very grateful to live in a country that tries to take care of its poor. But the challenge is, these government programs that were meant to help families through a crisis have become a lifestyle. These programs have facilitated dysfunctional families and undermined the need for a father and provider in the home. Such programs often lead to multi-generation, government-assisted cultures of poverty, in which poverty becomes an identity and thus a way of life.

> I am very grateful to live in a country that tries to take care of its poor. But the challenge is, these government programs that were meant to help families through a crisis have become a lifestyle.

Two Types of Poverty

To help us understand our situation, let me draw a contrast between two different types of poverty. I have been to many developing nations where people have lived in abject poverty for generations, with children literally starving to death in the arms of their parents. I have also visited many of the ghettos of America, where people are barely alive, often surviving on just a welfare check. Although these impoverished situations may seem similar on the surface, they are actually very different cultures of destitution.

The enormous differentiation between these two conditions can be summed up in a couple of words: *potential* and *possibility*. Let me explain it like this: If you grow up starving and impoverished in Mozambique, Africa, there is literally nowhere for you to go to escape the situation. The fact is, you have no transportation, no money and no job, and there is no place you know of where people are doing any better than the condition you are in.

On the other hand, if you grow up in the slums of Detroit, Michigan, you can get a bus ticket and be out of the ghetto in 30 minutes. The question is, Why don't you leave? Why don't you grab your stuff and catch a bus to a new neighborhood? Especially when that middle-class neighborhood is often just a few miles away. What, exactly, keeps you in the ghetto? It's likely that your family has been living in such conditions for generations, maybe even in the same destitute neighborhood. Yet literally, they have often never ventured outside the cage of poverty, have never gotten up one day and said, "I can do better than this." *Never, ever!* The question is, *Why?*

This is a complex inquiry that many experts have investigated and debated for decades. There are social conditions that make it very difficult for people to break out of the poverty barrier. I certainly don't want to be dogmatic in my approach to systemic poverty or to the outright prejudice that some people face every day. There are real educational restraints and funding disparities that must be dealt with in order to bring equality to every ethnic group and to people with disabilities. Truly, there are people in my country and other nations who have been victimized, reduced, marginalized and even murdered. Furthermore, I don't want to point the finger of judgment at people who have struggled to break free from the grip of destitution.

> **King Solomon spoke to the responsibility that fathers have to sow seeds of prosperity into their children's lives. He laid the practical responsibility of family prosperity squarely on the shoulders of fatherhood!**

Yet I do want to point out that so much (if not most) of American poverty is rooted in fatherlessness and perpetuated by the victim spirit that grows in the seedbed of abandonment and disconnection. King Solomon spoke to the responsibility that fathers have to sow seeds of prosperity into their children's lives. He wrote, "House and wealth are an inheritance from fathers" (Proverbs 19:14). Solomon laid the practical responsibility of family prosperity squarely on the shoulders of fatherhood!

The truth is that the responsibility of fatherhood lingers long after our children have left our homes. In fact, we fathers are tasked with helping fund our children's pilgrimage into adulthood. This is most often expressed through the word *inheritance*, which is a major theme throughout the book of Proverbs, and throughout the rest of the Bible, for that matter. Even the story of the prodigal son we covered earlier is rooted in a young man who asked his father for his inheritance and then wasted it on prostitutes. The story's revelation is *not* that the sons each had an inheritance. The moral of the story is the father's forgiveness for his sons. The audience Jesus was speaking to assumed the inheritance part of the story, since legacy was deeply ingrained in Jewish culture.

So many Scriptures reinforce the culture of inheritance. Here is another one that stands a man up against a wall and points a finger right in his chest: "A good man leaves an inheritance to his children's children" (Proverbs 13:22). There it is again—a noble man's challenge to step up to the plate and build an on-ramp to financial and spiritual wealth for his kids.

My Experience

My father was only 24 years old when he drowned. He was a good man, but he was just getting started in life. He had no life insurance policy or retirement package. Consequently, my mother was left penniless, with two small children to feed and care for. She was broke, scared and alone.

As a result, growing up I never heard a single conversation about inheritance or legacy. Nor did anyone ever take me aside and instruct me about my responsibility for the next generation (although later on in life, my mother was very generous with my family and helped us during tough seasons, as she was able). It never happened! But that all changed in 2004, in an encounter I had with the Lord. I was lying on the floor, praying in the Alabaster Prayer House at Bethel Church, when all of a sudden I was thrust a hundred years into the future in a vision. (Strange sounding . . . I understand, and I've told this story before, in my book

> **Growing up, I never heard a single conversation about inheritance or legacy. Nor did anyone ever take me aside and instruct me about my responsibility for the next generation.**

Heavy Rain, but it bears repeating in this context.) I found myself standing next to an old man in the living room of a beautiful, massive mansion. I could see the elderly man perfectly, but he couldn't see me. It seemed as if it was Thanksgiving or something. The smell of pies baking in the oven filled the house, and the excitement of a large family gathering was in the air. The adults talked and laughed as the kids played.

The elderly gentleman, encircled by several generations of family, was enthusiastically telling stories, mostly musing over the past, as old men often do. But then something happened. The tone of his voice changed and his facial expression grew serious, as if he was about to share something of great importance with them. Tears formed in his eyes as he looked off into the distance, as though he was trying to recall some ancient secret. The entire room grew silent as the rest of the family joined in the gathering. Everyone was leaning in to hear the words gracefully flowing from the old man's lips.

He began to speak to the gathered family about their noble roots and their royal heritage, staring into the eyes of each one present as if he was searching for greatness in their souls. He spoke of the huge sacrifice their forefathers had paid to obtain such favor, wealth and influence with God and man. But it was what he did next that stunned me. He pointed to a majestic stone fireplace that rose about thirty feet to a vaulted ceiling. I turned my gaze toward the fireplace mantle, where a large, beautiful portrait of Kathy and me hung. I was breathless as he finished his exhortation: "All of this began with your great-great-great-grandmother and great-great-great-grandfather!"

I instantly came out of the vision, and I was struggling to gather my thoughts. I heard a Voice speak to my spirit: *Your children's children's children are depending on you leaving them a world in revival. You are no longer to live for a ministry. From this day forward, you are to live to leave a legacy!*

What Now?

To be honest, I had *no idea* what to do or how to think about the experience I had. By now, you know my story. I am an overachiever. I am a simple man who has wrestled his way through life, trudged through intense obstacles, overcome my own father's death when I was three. I've had two nervous breakdowns and gone through the loss of our four businesses that took twenty long, hard years to build, the loss of our house that we built in the woods and the loss of all of our wealth. Kathy and I literally had to completely rebuild our entire financial world at 45 years of age. I am a survivor!

> **Kathy and I felt such a strong conviction that the Lord wanted us to take a step of faith and do something practical, radical and relevant regarding inheritance for our kids.**

Yet after my legacy experience, Kathy and I felt such a strong conviction that the Lord wanted us to take a step of faith and do something practical, radical and relevant regarding inheritance for our kids. At the time, we had seven grandkids (we have ten grandkids now, and one great-grandson), so we decided to open a bank account in each of their names and put $50 a month in their account for their future. Although it wasn't much, it was a huge sacrifice for us in those days because we really didn't have the money. Yet we knew God was challenging us to believe Him for financial miracles.

Consequently, our meager step of faith to bless the next generation paid off as Jesus so blessed us! On a salary of just $2,400 a month, we paid off and/or were forgiven the $1.8 million debt from our failed business, in just three years!

There Must Be More

This $50 per grandchild per month was a great start, but we wanted to do more, do something that would affect the eternity of the generations to come . . . the generations we wouldn't meet on this side of the veil of forever. We began praying and dreaming about how we could take what we have learned about God, life, love and pain and share it with our great-great-great-grandchildren, people who are yet to be born.

Moses said, "The secret things belong to the LORD our God, but the things revealed belong to us and to our sons forever" (Deuteronomy 29:29). This verse helped challenge us to make our revelation an inheritance, kind of like passing our spiritual "intellectual property" down to our kids. I decided that I would write my next book specifically to my great-grandkids, but still let the public read it. It's the book I just mentioned, called *Heavy Rain*. It's a book about the outpouring of the Holy Spirit that transforms people and culture. This is my most revelatory work . . . my best attempt at predicting the future state of the world from a Kingdom perspective, a world my descendants will hopefully be experiencing by the time they read the book. Here is the *Heavy Rain* dedication:

> I dedicate this book to my children's children's children's children. Though we will not meet until we get to heaven, I wanted you to know that I had you in mind as I wrote every word of this book, and I continue to hold you in my heart. You will become the answer to my prayers and the fulfillment of my prophecies. By the time you read this book, I will be watching you from heaven (see Hebrews 12:1).[2]

Last year, Kathy also wrote a book titled *The Good, the God and the Ugly: The Inside Story of a Supernatural Family* (Chosen, 2021). She wanted to leave a written record of our family's supernatural exploits in Jesus to the generations to come. This was her love gift, her spiritual inheritance for our children's children's children, who are yet to be born.

The challenge I see as I pen the words of this book is that many who will grace these pages have not been fathered themselves. They are left alone to find their way through the jungle of life, often with their families in tow, with no idea how to lead them on a practical basis, much less leave a legacy. Furthermore, the pressure of the here-and-now is so intense at times that it's hard to have the time or emotional capacity even to think about the hereafter.

Yet healthy and holistic fatherhood begins by setting aside the urgent to give attention to the important, the vital and the significant. These are the ways of honorable men, men who become noble fathers and thus shatter the iron bars of the orphan spirit. They rescue society from the jaws of a self-absorbed, self-centered, narcissistic environment and bulldoze new mindsets into the wanting, willing, humble and hopeful.

EPIC
TAKEAWAYS

- A dysfunctional ecosystem: The cycle of poverty is exacerbated by the guilt and shame of prodigal fathers, who distance themselves and disconnect from their families. They then feel more guilt and shame, and then they isolate themselves further . . . and the cycle continues.
- Facilitating the dysfunction: Governmental programs that were meant to help families through a crisis have become a lifestyle through undermining the need for a father and provider in the home.
- Poverty at its root: So much (if not most) of American poverty is rooted in fatherlessness and perpetuated by the victim spirit that grows in the seedbed of abandonment and disconnection.
- An assumed inheritance: Fathers leaving an inheritance to their children was a given in Jewish culture. The prodigal son's story is rooted in his father's forgiveness, not in his father leaving him a legacy. The inheritance part was already understood by the parable's hearers!
- Proverbs 13:22: "A good man leaves an inheritance to his children's children." A noble man's challenge is to step up to the plate and build an on-ramp to financial and spiritual wealth for his kids.
- Life is about leaving a legacy: In my vision of the elderly man and his family, the Lord told me, *Your children's children's children are depending on you leaving them a world in revival. You are no longer to live for a ministry. From this day forward, you are to live to leave a legacy!*
- Deuteronomy 29:29: "The secret things belong to the Lord our God, but the things revealed belong to us and to our sons forever." This challenged Kathy and me to take what we have learned about

God, life, love and pain and share it with our great-great-great-grandchildren, people who are yet to be born.

- Inheriting revelation: Make your revelation an inheritance by passing your spiritual "intellectual property" down to your kids and grandkids. They will then become the answer to your prayers and the fulfillment of your prophecies.

SIXTEEN

The Malachi Mandate

I GATHERED BETHEL'S LEADERSHIP TEAM, a group of about seventy people, for a strategy meeting regarding the challenges we were facing as a church and a movement. I stepped up to the front of the room to address the group and looked down at my notes, which read, "Talk about transition." I started to speak, but before I could utter any words, the Lord said, *Bethel is not going through a transition; it's going through a metamorphosis. Transition is the process of going from one season to another, but metamorphosis is not about changing seasons, but about changing you . . . the people of God.*

Surprised by the interruption, I repeated the Lord's revelation to the team as everybody just sat there looking surprised. I continued with what I was hearing: *The caterpillar is attached to the earth, but it must endure the dark season of the cocoon to transition to a butterfly, and be devoted to the heavens.*

Over the next few weeks, I realized that this prophetic declaration wasn't just for Bethel Church; it was relevant for the nations! The revelation began to unfold with specific details about the meaning of the word *metamorphosis* and the profound effect it would have on the nations. I discovered that caterpillars spend about two weeks in the cocoon, where they literally liquefy as they morph into a butterfly. If the cocoon is prematurely opened, the butterfly will die, or won't be able to fly. It's the stress and strain it experiences in the cocoon exodus that cause the butterfly to gain the strength it needs to fly.

I came to realize that society has entered a cocoon of darkness, which can cause us to feel powerless, lonely and depressed. This metamorphosis feels like Elijah's cave experience, in which he had just destroyed Jezebel's 450 prophets of Baal and had turned Israel back to God in defiance of the wicked king Ahab. We talked about this back in chapter 2, but here's the rest of the story. The day after Elijah's great conquest, Ahab's wife, Queen Jezebel, went nuts because she was the one who had been leading Israel to follow Baal. Thus she vowed to kill Elijah: "Then Jezebel sent a messenger to Elijah, saying, 'So may the gods do to me and even more, if I do not make your life as the life of one of them by tomorrow about this time'" (1 Kings 19:2). Her threats so freaked Elijah out that he asked God to kill him! It's as if the guy had a breakdown of some kind and lost sight of his powerful identity and his profound calling. He ran and hid in a cave, shaking in his proverbial boots. Then God showed up at the cave, and Elijah watched Him display His mighty power:

> The word of the LORD came to him, and He said to him, "What are you doing here, Elijah?" He said, "I have been very zealous for the LORD, the God of hosts; for the sons of Israel have forsaken Your covenant, torn down Your altars and killed Your prophets with the sword. And I alone am left; and they seek my life, to take it away."
>
> So He said, "Go forth and stand on the mountain before the LORD." And behold, the LORD was passing by! And a great and strong wind was rending the mountains and breaking in pieces the rocks before the LORD; but the LORD was not in the wind. And after the wind an earthquake, but the LORD was not in the earthquake. After the earthquake a fire, but the LORD was not in the fire; and after the fire a sound of a gentle blowing. When Elijah heard it, he wrapped his face in his mantle and went out and stood in the entrance of the cave. And behold, a voice came to him and said, "What are you doing here, Elijah?" Then he said, "I have been very zealous for the LORD, the God of hosts; for the sons of Israel have forsaken Your covenant, torn

down Your altars and killed Your prophets with the sword. And I alone am left; and they seek my life, to take it away."

1 Kings 19:9–14

Elijah was in such despair, and yet 24 hours earlier this powerful prophet had called fire down from heaven with a short, two-line prayer in the sight of all of Israel. The supernatural fire consumed the wet sacrifice on the altar and even "licked up the water that was in the trench" he had dug around it (1 Kings 18:38).

> **The Father-to-son talk at the opening of the cave transformed the cavern into a cocoon, out of which Elijah emerged from his despair with a new perspective on his ministry.**

The Father-to-son talk at the opening of the cave transformed the cavern into a cocoon, out of which Elijah emerged from his despair with a new perspective on his ministry. God clarified his mission and then gave him the instruction to find and anoint a spiritual son named Elisha to follow him. It's important to emphasize here that God's answer to Elijah's irrational fear and suicidal condition was that he needed to get back to his ministry mandate of anointing kings, and become a father to a spiritual son named Elisha. Here are God's specific instructions to His friend and prophet:

> The LORD said to him, "Go, return on your way to the wilderness of Damascus, and when you have arrived, you shall anoint Hazael king over Aram; and Jehu the son of Nimshi you shall anoint king over Israel; and Elisha the son of Shaphat of Abel-meholah you shall anoint as prophet in your place."
>
> 1 Kings 19:15–16

The Next Generation of Prophets

Elijah left the cave of his cocoon and met Elisha in a field where he was farming for his father. Elijah threw his mantle on him and then walked away without a word. (A weird greeting, I'd say.) Elisha seemed to get it, though, as he immediately sacrificed the 24 oxen he was plowing with and followed Elijah.

It's stunning to me that Elisha knew instinctively that he had to leave his natural inheritance to receive his spiritual one. He left his father's house and killed the oxen on the way out the door. Do you understand what happened here? Elisha burned the bridge to his old, caterpillar way of life. Now he had nothing to fall back on; it was climb or die.

No wonder God chose Elisha to take Elijah's place. Elisha did instinctively in faith what was never asked of him. He was a Spirit-led man (see 1 Kings 19:19–21).

From there, Elisha followed Elijah for eight years as Elijah discipled him in his call as a prophet and fathered him in his life as a son. Then suddenly, in a wild turn of events, the Lord told Elijah that He was going to take him up to heaven in a whirlwind. This made him one of only two people in the history of the world never to die. (Enoch was the other person who went to heaven without dying.)

What's exciting here is that Elijah went into that cave as a lonely prophet, believing he was the only prophet left in Israel. But he emerged from that cocoon as a father. Just eight short years after leaving that cave of gloom and doom, Elijah was surrounded by spiritual sons referred to as "the sons of the prophets." Over those few years, Elijah created a prophetic community in which gifted prophets became his sons, and the entire prophetic movement became a family!

Somehow, when the time came for Elijah to leave, the whole company of prophets knew by divine revelation that he was about to make a dramatic exit to heaven. It's evident that revelation had become a family affair as God had anointed a relationally connected team of prophets to share together in the mysteries of His Kingdom. Elijah and Elisha traveled from city to city one day in something like a victory tour, or maybe it was meant to be more of a farewell excursion. Either way, everywhere they went they encountered more "sons of the prophets," and these prophets kept announcing to Elisha that God was taking Elijah to heaven that very day (see 2 Kings 2:1–7).

The funny thing is, while these two prophets were on their farewell tour together, Elijah tried to ditch Elisha several times throughout their daylong journey, but Elisha refused to leave his side. This is where the story gets crazy. Read it for yourself:

> Then Elijah took his cloak and rolled it up and struck the water, and the water was parted to the one side and to the other, till the two of them could go over on dry ground.
>
> When they had crossed, Elijah said to Elisha, "Ask what I shall do for you, before I am taken from you." And Elisha said, "Please let there be a double portion of your spirit on me." And he said, "You have asked a hard thing; yet, if you see me as I am being taken from you, it shall be so for you, but if you do not see me, it shall not be so." And as they still went on and talked, behold, chariots of fire and horses of fire separated the two of them. And Elijah went up by a whirlwind into heaven. And Elisha saw it and he cried, "My father, my father! The chariots of Israel and its horsemen!" And he saw him no more.
>
> Then he took hold of his own clothes and tore them in two pieces. And he took up the cloak of Elijah that had fallen from him and went back and stood on the bank of the Jordan. Then he took the cloak of Elijah that had fallen from him and struck the water, saying, "Where is the LORD, the God of Elijah?" And when he had struck the water, the water was parted to the one side and to the other, and Elisha went over.
>
> 2 Kings 2:8–14 ESV

I have often wondered why Elijah was trying to ditch Elisha on the final day of his Old Testament journey. Now I realize that Elijah was testing Elisha's desire for relational connection. He knew that for Elisha to keep the family of prophets healthy after his departure, relational connection would have to be his highest priority. A double portion of his spirit could only be contained in the wineskin of a healthy community of fathers and sons!

After their multicity tour was complete, Elijah went up to heaven in a whirlwind, and Elisha proclaimed, "My father, my father! The chariots of Israel and its horsemen!" Elisha didn't say, "My prophet, my prophet!" Can you see it? Elijah's last prophetic mandate before he left the earth behind in a flaming chariot, under the *Old Covenant*, was to find and father spiritual sons who would take his place. How profound is this? Suddenly, Malachi's mandate makes perfect sense. Let's look at it one more time:

> Behold, I will send you Elijah the prophet before the great and awesome day of the LORD comes. And he will turn the hearts of fathers to their children and the hearts of children to their fathers, lest I come and strike the land with a decree of utter destruction.
>
> Malachi 4:5–6 ESV

Now, Elijah's first prophetic mandate in the *New Covenant* is the restoration of fatherhood and the reconciliation of the generations. Who better to ignite a worldwide family reformation in the last days than a prophet who turned Israel back to God with signs and wonders, and yet knew the deep despair of fatherlessness because he lived it himself?

The New-Covenant Elijah

The next time we see Elijah, it's in the New Testament, standing on the Mount of Transfiguration, talking with Moses and Jesus (see Matthew 17:1–8). Thus, the ministry that was mandated in Malachi was initiated in Matthew, since Elijah never died! When the meeting was over, the disciples walked down from the mountain with Jesus, and as you can imagine, they had a ton of questions. Interestingly, none of their questions were about Moses, the audible voice of God or the shining garments of Christ. They were all about Elijah. They asked Jesus, "Why then do the scribes say that Elijah must come first?" (Matthew 17:10). Look what Jesus replied:

> And He answered and said, "Elijah is coming and will restore all things; but I say to you that Elijah already came, and they did not recognize him, but did to him whatever they wished. So also the Son of Man is going to suffer at their hands." Then the disciples understood that He had spoken to them about John the Baptist.
>
> Matthew 17:11–13

Earlier in Matthew's gospel, Jesus had said, "If you are willing to accept it, John himself is Elijah who was to come" (Matthew 11:14). All of this was prophesied years before by the angel Gabriel, when he met Zacharias, the father of John the Baptist, in the Temple. Gabriel prophesied John's birth and divine call before John was conceived, saying,

He will turn many of the sons of Israel back to the Lord their God. It is he who will go as a forerunner before Him in the spirit and power of Elijah, *to turn the hearts of the fathers back to the children*, and the disobedient to the attitude of the righteous, so as to make ready a people prepared for the Lord.

Luke 1:16–17, emphasis added

What's noteworthy here is that the priests asked John the Baptist, "Are you Elijah?" And he said, "I am not. . . . I am a voice of one crying in the wilderness, 'Make straight the way of the Lord,' as Isaiah the prophet said" (John 1:21, 23). It's interesting that Jesus said that John was Elijah, and Gabriel said that John would come in the spirit and power of Elijah, yet John never performed a single miracle. (Or did he?)

Was John Elijah? The answer is *yes* and *no*. John wasn't the person of Elijah, but he was the personification of Elijah—meaning that John was carrying the same mandate of generational reconciliation. Like Elijah, who turned all of Israel away from Baal and back to Jehovah, John the Baptist turned an entire generation back to God. But as Jesus pointed out, John *was* the Elijah of the first century. Yet Elijah is still coming to restore all things (read Matthew 17:10–12 again).

A few years after the resurrection, Peter and John healed a lame man at the Gate Beautiful, which caused a large crowd of over three thousand people to gather. Peter stood up and began preaching to them, resulting in three thousand souls saved. Take a close look at the last point of Peter's message:

And likewise, all the prophets who have spoken, from Samuel and his successors onward, also announced these days. It is you who are the sons of the prophets and of the covenant which God made with your fathers, saying to Abraham, "And in your seed all the families of the earth shall be blessed."

Acts 3:24–25

Did you catch it? Peter said, "It is you who are the sons of the prophets and of the covenant which God made with your fathers" (verse 25). The mantle that was on Elijah, which was passed to Elisha, and was personified in John the Baptist, and was prophesied by Malachi, *is on you!* You are part of the prophetic family; you are the "sons of the prophets" who are carrying the spirit of Elijah, with the Malachi Mandate to restore *all*

> **The mantle that was on Elijah, which was passed to Elisha, and was personified in John the Baptist, and was prophesied by Malachi, *is on you!***

things—especially the restoration of fatherhood in the lives of sons and daughters. God is calling us to wear the mantle for our nations and once again reconcile the generations.

We must build a bridge over the gaping chasm between fathers and their lineage; otherwise, this relational gorge will insulate the blessing to one generation and undermine the inheritance that God designed to grow and increase from generation to generation. Thus, the mandate of the reconciliation of fathers and children is powerful for so many reasons. But most importantly, it reinstates the power of the inheritance.

This truth is highlighted in the book of Luke, when Jesus tells a story about a man who planted a vineyard and left it to his servants. The owner sent slaves to collect his share of the harvest every year, but the vineyard servants beat up the slaves and refused to give the landlord his cut of the harvest. Here is the rest of the story:

> The owner of the vineyard said, "What shall I do? I will send my beloved son; perhaps they will respect him." But when the vine-growers saw him, they reasoned with one another, saying, "This is the heir; let us kill him so that the inheritance will be ours."
>
> Luke 20:13–14

The vineyard represents God's Kingdom, and the servants are the religious leaders who stole the Kingdom from God Himself. The son is Jesus, whom they will kill to keep the inheritance for themselves. Here it is, the climax of the parable: The war is over the *inheritance*!

Jezebel Then and Now

Jezebel was the archenemy of Elijah in the Old Covenant, as we saw already. She sacrificed children on the altars of Baal, and she instituted immorality and witchcraft into the very fabric of Israeli culture. She had Naboth, her neighbor, stoned to death to steal his land, his inheritance from his father, just so Ahab could have a vegetable garden by his palace. And somehow, that wicked witch found her way into the New Testament. Her spirit is again at war with believers, attempting to destroy families and seduce the Church into immorality. Jesus said in Revelation 2:20, "I have this against you, that you tolerate the woman Jezebel, who calls herself a prophetess, and she teaches and leads My bond-servants astray so that they commit acts of immorality and eat things sacrificed to idols."

In the Old Testament, Elijah prophesied the death of Jezebel. But it was Elisha who anointed Jehu king over Israel and instructed him to destroy that witch, on the property of Jezreel, the very land she had stolen from Naboth (see 2 Kings 9). In the New Covenant we are told, "Our struggle is not against flesh and blood, but against the rulers, against the powers, against the world forces of this darkness, against the spiritual forces of wickedness in the heavenly places" (Ephesians 6:12). Although we are not in a fight with a person, make no mistake about it, we are in a war with the spirit of that wicked witch Jezebel, a spirit that is trying to divide the generations in order to destroy the multigenerational inheritance that is passed *up* from generation to generation.

Think about how deceptive and powerful the Jezebel spirit is. The day after Elijah's greatest victory, in which he became one of the most renowned heroes in Israeli history, he was suddenly steeped in a demonic delusion—this man who had demonstrated power over the weather (he stopped the rain for three and a half years), and who had authority over the elements (he called fire down from heaven), and who destroyed the witchcraft that was entrenched in the very fabric of the nation, and who singlehandedly turned the heart of Israel back to Jehovah in one day. The Jezebel spirit was so deceptive in Elijah's life that he literally forgot his great victories and was convinced that he had lost to Jezebel and her band of evil false prophets.

I see the same Jezebel spirit at work in our nations today. It is manifest in so many believers who are living a delusional life in which this spirit redefines their victories as defeats, convinces them that their ministry is

> We carry the root of a legacy mindset; we are people who live to empower the generations to come.

meaningless and persuades them into believing that the devil is winning the world and that they are powerless to stop him. But as 1 John 4:4 tells us, greater is He who is in us than he who is in the world! We are the Elijah generation, the sons of the prophets, called to carry out this Malachi Mandate to disciple the nations. We carry the root of a legacy mindset; we are people who live to empower the generations to come.

The Vision

This is such a powerful revelation, but something happened to me in a government prayer meeting in early 2019 that made it even more relevant to our generation. I was leading about seventy people in prayer for the fatherlessness factor in our nations when suddenly I had a profound vision. I saw boys and men leaving their houses and filling the streets in complete despair. At first, there were just a few of them walking the streets alone, but little by little the crowd grew to hundreds, and then to thousands, and then to millions. Instinctively, kind of like birds who fly south in the winter, these men were making their way toward various stadiums, as if there was an inner voice compelling or wooing them to come.

The vision shifted as I drew near to one stadium, and I could hear my son Jason's voice welcoming the men into the arena, the way the father had welcomed the prodigal son home in the Luke 15 story we talked about. Each man entered the stadium in ragged clothes, his face covered in shame and his heart broken in abandonment. But as these men came into the arena, their faces began to glow, their hearts started to sing and their spirits came alive!

Suddenly I heard the Lord shout, *The Malachi Mandate! The Malachi Mandate!* He then continued, *Behold, I will send you Elijah the prophet before the great and awesome day of the LORD comes. And he will turn the hearts of fathers to their children and the hearts of children to their fathers, lest I come and strike the land with a decree of utter destruction.*

Then I heard Jason say, "Welcome, men! Today we are going to teach you how to be men, and lead you in the rite of passage!"

I was stunned by the vision. Weeping, I took out my phone and began to text Jason while I was still in the vision. I described the vision to him in detail. He immediately responded to my text with, "Dad, I had the same vision a few months ago! I know this is God."

A few months later, a team of prophetic people in a ministry called Aqua Regia, led by Lindsey Reiman, got together in what's called a double-blind prophetic session. In these sessions, prophetic teams are given a number instead of a name, so they have no idea whom they are prophesying to. Several of them pray alone over the same number, and then a prophetic journal is compiled and given to the person that number represented. My prophetic journal was ninety pages long, and what emerged from its pages was nothing less than profound! First, they saw me in "the Situation Room" of the White House, discussing the issues that face our country. One of them then added to the journal, "The stadium is next. I see a venue like the Rose Bowl or the L.A. Coliseum. As you have counseled privately in the Situation Room, there are issues that need addressing publicly. This is a rally cry, bringing to light issues and providing solutions and hope. Late spring or early summer of 2021 is your target date."

> "Welcome, men! Today we are going to teach you how to be men, and lead you in the rite of passage!"

Within months, I was invited by several congresspeople to do leadership seminars to help them find solutions to America's toughest situations. I met with this group of congresspeople five times, sharing in each three-hour session the root issues that are plaguing America, and explaining that *all* of these issues could be traced back to fatherlessness.

BraveCo

While I was meeting with the congresspeople, Jason gathered several strong spiritual leaders around him and launched a powerful men's movement called BraveCo (meaning a brave company of men). The BraveCo movement is commissioned to carry the Malachi Mandate to the nations.

In 2021 (the target date in my prophetic journal), BraveCo, in partnership with Limitless, had its first stadium gathering at the Banc of California Stadium in Los Angeles! Since then, Jason has gathered a team of spiritual fathers together and has created a discipleship strategy and structure to begin to father a fatherless generation. Soon, hundreds of thousands of men will be gathering in groups all around the nation to learn how boys become men, and how men become fathers. The *dream* is alive!

In the midst of my writing this book, my granddaughter Mesha gave birth to my first great-grandson. She had an encounter with the Lord, and He told her to name him Malachi.

Brian and Jenn Johnson adopted a baby at the same time, and the Lord told them to call him Malachi.

Twenty years ago, my son Jason and his wife, Heather, were pregnant with their first child, my first grandson. During the pregnancy, I had a dream and the Lord told me, *You will name your grandson Elijah, and he will be a prophet to this generation.* I told the kids about this encounter, and they used the name.

Now my oldest grandson is named Elijah, and my youngest and first great-grandson is named Malachi! You just can't make this stuff up!

It's Our Time

This is exciting, but the challenge is much greater than a single church or one movement can solve by itself. The heart of the Malachi Mandate must be expressed through ten thousand BraveCo-like gatherings, in which men emerge from the stadiums of empowerment and rescue this generation from the Jezebel spirit. We must put a stop to the storms of disconnection and abandonment and pull this generation back to the shores of healthy and holistic fatherhood.

While I was finishing the last chapter of this book, a friend of mine named Andy Mason sent me a prophetic word out of Isaiah 58. Andy said, "The Lord told me to tell you that this verse is for you: 'Those from among you will rebuild the ancient ruins; you will raise up the age-old foundations; and you will be called the repairer of the breach, the restorer of the streets in which to dwell'" (Isaiah 58:12).

I love the verse, but I was also stunned by the context and felt so strongly that I was to close this book with Isaiah's exhortation to us:

> **We must put a stop to the storms of disconnection and abandonment, and pull this generation back to the shores of healthy and holistic fatherhood.**

Cry loudly, do not hold back; raise your voice like a trumpet, and declare to My people their transgression and to the house of Jacob their sins. Yet they seek Me day by day and delight to know My ways, as a nation that has done righteousness and has not forsaken the ordinance of their God. They ask Me for just decisions, they delight in the nearness of God. "Why have we fasted and You do not see? Why have we humbled ourselves and You do not notice?" Behold, on the day of your fast you find your desire, and drive hard all your workers. Behold, you fast for contention and strife and to strike with a wicked fist. You do not fast like you do today to make your voice heard on high. Is it a fast like this which I choose, a day for a man to humble himself? Is it for bowing one's head like a reed and for spreading out sackcloth and ashes as a bed? Will you call this a fast, even an acceptable day to the LORD? Is this not the fast which I choose, to loosen the bonds of wickedness, to undo the bands of the yoke, and to let the oppressed go free and break every yoke? Is it not to divide your bread with the hungry and bring the homeless poor into the house; when you see the naked, to cover him; and not to hide yourself from your own flesh? Then your light will break out like the dawn, and your recovery will speedily spring forth; and your righteousness will go before you; the glory of the LORD will be your rear guard. Then you will call, and the LORD will answer; you will cry, and He will say, "Here I am." If you remove the yoke from your midst, the pointing of the finger and speaking wickedness, and if you give yourself to the hungry and satisfy the desire of the afflicted, then your light will rise in darkness and your gloom will become like midday. And the LORD will continually guide you, and satisfy your desire in scorched places, and give strength to your bones; and you will be like a watered garden, and like a spring of water whose waters do not fail. Those from among you will rebuild the ancient ruins; you will raise up the age-old foundations; and you will be called the repairer of the breach, the restorer of the streets in which to dwell.

Isaiah 58:1–12

This passage begins a little Old Testament harshly, but it ends with a wonderful promise. Yet what captured my heart was the fact that God's rebuke was this: "Yet they seek Me day by day and delight to know My ways, as a nation that has done righteousness and has not forsaken the ordinance of their God. They ask Me for just decisions, they delight in the nearness of God" (verse 2). The Lord went on to point out here that His people's passion for His presence didn't translate into helping the homeless, the fatherless, the poor and/or the broken.

God goes on to pronounce over Israel one of the most powerful *conditional* promises ever declared over a nation in human history. The question to us all is, Will we qualify for the blessing by meeting the conditions of this prophetic mandate, and thus shift the course of the nations toward wholeness?

Andy Mason's answer from the book of Isaiah rings in my ear: "Those from among you will rebuild the ancient ruins; you will raise up the age-old foundations; and you will be called the repairer of the breach, the restorer of the streets in which to dwell." The mantle has fallen to us. Now the only question that remains is, Will the fathers of this generation take up Elijah's mantle of generational reconciliation? Will they rise up and answer the call of God to embrace the Malachi Mandate and turn their hearts toward home and family?

EPIC
TAKEAWAYS

- A *metamorphosis*: A *transition* is the process of going from one season to another, but a *metamorphosis* is not about changing seasons, but about changing us, the people of God.

- A cocoon of darkness: Society has entered a cocoon of darkness, which can cause us to feel powerless, lonely and depressed. We need to go through a metamorphosis that changes us as people, fathers and nations.

- Elijah's cocoon: The cave the prophet hid from Jezebel in actually became a cocoon out of which he emerged from his despair with a new perspective on his ministry.

- John the Baptist and Elijah: John wasn't the person of Elijah, but he was the personification of Elijah—meaning that John was carrying the same mandate of generational reconciliation. Like Elijah, who turned all of Israel away from Baal and back to Jehovah, John the Baptist turned an entire generation back to God.

- Passing the mantle: We are part of the "sons of the prophets" who are carrying the spirit of Elijah, and who have the Malachi Mandate to restore *all things*. God is therefore calling us to wear the mantle for our nation and once again reconcile the generations.

- Jezebel's war: The spirit of Jezebel is working to destroy the multigenerational inheritance that is passed *up* from generation to generation. But we who carry the Malachi Mandate carry the root of a legacy mindset; we are people who live to empower the generations to come.

- The stadium vision: I saw men making their way in droves to stadiums where they were welcomed and taught how to be men, and where their spirits came alive!

- BraveCo: The dream or vision of the stadiums is coming to pass in the BraveCo movement, spearheaded by my son Jason. This movement is commissioned to carry the Malachi Mandate to the

215

nations, as men emerge from the stadiums of empowerment and rescue this generation from the Jezebel spirit.

- Reaching the shore: We must put a stop to the storms of disconnection and abandonment and pull this generation back to the shores of healthy and holistic fatherhood.

- A final prophetic word: "Those from among you will rebuild the ancient ruins; you will raise up the age-old foundations; and you will be called the repairer of the breach, the restorer of the streets in which to dwell" (Isaiah 58:12).

NOTES

Chapter 1 Where It All Began

1. I tell a longer version of this story as "The Parable of the Ring" in the book I wrote with my son Jason, *Moral Revolution: The Naked Truth about Sexual Purity* (Chosen, 2012). *Moral Revolution* focuses specifically on helping people restore purity in their lives and is a great tool for those who need help in this area. I wanted to recap the story of the ring here, however, and introduce you to the kids I told it to, as we look at the far-reaching effects of fatherlessness today.

Chapter 2 Where Have All the Fathers Gone?

1. You can read more about the story of my breakdown and healing in *Spirit Wars: Winning the Invisible Battle against Sin and the Enemy* (Chosen, 2012), a book for anyone fighting for freedom and peace of mind.

2. The Fatherless Generation website is the source of many of the statistics I share on fatherlessness throughout this book. You can find it at https://thefatherlessgeneration .wordpress.com. See in particular the link to Statistics. I also want to mention that part of the challenge right now in citing statistics on fatherlessness is that some of the studies done in decades past are no longer done now, because it is politically incorrect to call a home with two mothers "fatherless"! The statistical data is therefore dated on purpose because the government and so many other entities have stopped doing such studies. At least that's my theory, because so much of the available data is twenty years old, and we know that the fatherlessness situation hasn't gotten better, but worse! I think that, because it has become politically incorrect to cite fatherless homes as dysfunctional, in our PC times there is therefore much less statistical data that is current.

3. Joseph Chamie, "Out-of-Wedlock Births Rise Worldwide," YaleGlobal Online, March 16, 2017, https://archive-yaleglobal.yale.edu/content/out-wedlock-births-rise-worldwide.

4. "Table 7: Nonmarital childbearing, by detailed race and Hispanic origin of mother, and maternal age: United States, selected years 1970–2010," cdc.gov "Health, United States 2011" web updates, https://www.cdc.gov/nchs/data/hus/2011/007.pdf.

5. "Parenting in America: 1. The American Family Today," Pew Research Center report, December 17, 2015, https://www.pewresearch.org/social-trends/2015/12/17/1-the-american -family-today/.

6. Annie E. Casey Foundation, Kids Count Data Center, "Children in Single-Parent Families by Race/Ethnicity," United Way of Central Oklahoma online, https://www.unitedwayokc.org /research/data-center/children-single-parent-families/.

Chapter 3 Living in a Feminized Society

1. Hebrew and Greek translations throughout are taken from my Accordance Bible Software's NAS Hebrew and Greek Dictionaries that are included with the NASB1995 group of program resources.

2. Cecilia Dhejne, Paul Lichtenstein, Marcus Boman, Anna L V Johansson, Niklas Långström, Mikael Landén, "Long-Term Follow-Up of Transsexual Persons Undergoing Sex Reassignment Surgery: Cohort Study in Sweden," PubMed.gov, February 22, 2011, https://pubmed.ncbi.nlm.nih.gov/21364939/. See also J. T. O. Cavanagh, A. J. Carson, M. Sharpe, S. M. Lawrie, "Psychological autopsy studies of suicide: a systematic review," Cambridge University Press online, April 10, 2003, https://www.cambridge.org/core /journals/psychological-medicine/article/abs/psychological-autopsy-studies-of-suicide -a-systematic-review/49EEDF1D29B26C270A2788275995FDEE.

3. Andrea Long Chu, "My New Vagina Won't Make Me Happy: And It Shouldn't Have To," *New York Times*, November 24, 2018, https://www.nytimes.com/2018/11/24/opinion /sunday/vaginoplasty-transgender-medicine.html.

Chapter 4 Toxic Masculinity?

1. *Wikipedia*, s.v. "Toxic masculinity," last modified November 28, 2021, https://en.wiki pedia.org/wiki/Toxic_masculinity.

2. Abilash Gopal, M.D., with Margot Loren, "Reviving Romeo: Reclaiming the male identity in the age of 'toxic masculinity,'" *No Sugar Pills Here* (blog), *Psychology Today*, June 5, 2019, https://www.psychologytoday.com/us/blog/no-sugar-pills-here/201906/reviving -romeo.

3. This elephant story is my retelling, but you can read the actual story by Father Gordon MacRae, "In the Absence of Fathers: A Story of Elephants and Men," on the Beyond These Stone Walls website, https://beyondthesestonewalls.com/blog/gordon-macrae/in-the-absence -of-fathers-a-story-of-elephants-and-men.

4. E. Ann Carson, Ph.D., "Prisoners in 2019," U.S. Department of Justice, Bureau of Justice Statistics, October 2020, https://bjs.ojp.gov/content/pub/pdf/p19.pdf. See also Wiki-pedia, s.v. "List of countries by incarceration rate," last modified December 5, 2021, https:// en.wikipedia.org/wiki/List_of_countries_by_incarceration_rate.

5. Lauren G. Beatty and Tracy L. Snell, "Profile of Prison Inmates, 2016," U.S. De-partment of Justice Special Report, December 2021, https://bjs.ojp.gov/content/pub/pdf /ppi16.pdf.

6. See The Fatherless Generation website's Statistics page, https://thefatherlessgeneration .wordpress.com/statistics/.

7. Ibid.

8. Ibid.

9. Ibid.

10. Ibid.

Chapter 5 The Rite of Passage

1. Chris Bruno, *Man Maker Project: Boys Are Born. Men Are Made* (Eugene, Ore.: Resource Publications, 2015), 19.
2. You can read more about this story in Malcolm Gladwell, *Blink: The Power of Thinking without Thinking* (New York: Little, Brown and Company, 2005), 68.
3. Bruno, *Man Maker Project*, 38.

Chapter 6 The Plight of Fatherless Daughters

1. Kris Vallotton and Jason Vallotton, *Moral Revolution: The Naked Truth about Sexual Purity* (Minneapolis: Chosen Books, 2012), 68–71.

Chapter 9 Sex and Culture

1. James Studnicki, John W. Fisher, and James L. Sherley, "Perceiving and Addressing the Pervasive Racial Disparity in Abortion," NCBI Resources online, PMC US National Library of Medicine, National Institutes of Health, August 18, 2020, https://www.ncbi.nlm.nih.gov /pmc/articles/PMC7436774/.
2. Anna Purna Kambhampaty, "Why Planned Parenthood Is Removing Founder Margaret Sanger's Name from a New York City Clinic," *Time* magazine online, July 21, 2020, https:// time.com/5869743/planned-parenthood-margaret-sanger/.

Chapter 12 Finding Fathers

1. Brené Brown, *Daring Greatly: How the Courage to Be Vulnerable Transforms the Way We Live, Love, Parent, and Lead* (New York: Avery, 2012), 34.
2. Greek and Hebrew translations throughout are taken from my Accordance Bible Software's NAS Hebrew and Greek Dictionaries that are included with the NASB1995 group of program resources.

Chapter 13 Spiritual Men

1. I'm quoting Guillermo Maldonado's words to the best of my memory from that powerful conference.

Chapter 15 Leaving a Legacy

1. Robert Rector, "How Welfare Undermines Marriage and What to Do about It," The Heritage Foundation Issue Brief no. 4302, November 17, 2014, http://thf_media.s3.amazon aws.com/2014/pdf/IB4302.pdf.
2. Kris Vallotton, *Heavy Rain: How to Flood Your World with God's Transforming Power*, rev. ed. (Minneapolis: Chosen Books, 2016), 9.

Kris Vallotton is the senior associate leader of Bethel Church in Redding, California, and the co-founder of Bethel School of Supernatural Ministry (BSSM) and Moral Revolution. Kris is a noted prophetic voice worldwide and a bestselling author. He has written more than a dozen books and training manuals to help prepare believers for life in the Kingdom. He is also a highly sought-after international speaker, equipping people to successfully fulfill their divine purpose.

Kris has a diverse background in business, counseling, consulting, pastoring and teaching. He loves both to teach the masses and to advise leaders one-on-one, utilizing his experience and his prophetic gift to assist world influencers in achieving their goals. He commonly provides counsel to governmental and business leaders on practical strategies for cultural transformation and has unique expertise in economies and building prosperous communities. He is also the author of a weekly blog on www.kris vallotton.com.

Kris has been happily married to his wife, Kathy, since 1975. They have four children, ten grandchildren and one great-grandson. Kathy has recently written her first book, *The Good, the God and the Ugly: The Inside Story of a Supernatural Family* (Chosen, 2021), which is filled with stories of the Vallotton family.

More from Kris Vallotton

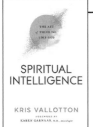

God invites you to bring your perspective into line with his—transforming your understanding and actually endowing you with spiritual intelligence. In this eye-opening book, Kris Vallotton explores how listening to the Holy Spirit and understanding what it means to have the mind of Christ will give you the capacity for life-transforming spiritual intelligence.

Spiritual Intelligence

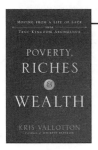

In this eye-opening study of what the Bible really says about money, poverty, riches, and wealth, Kris Vallotton will shake up what you thought you knew, showing that Kingdom prosperity always begins from the inside out. When you learn to cultivate a mindset of abundance, you will begin to experience the wealth of heaven in every area of your life.

Poverty, Riches and Wealth